Baseball Legends of Brooklyn's Green-Wood Cemetery

James Creighton Jr. revolutionized the position of the baseball pitcher in the 19th century and was the game's first true star. Upon his tragic death in 1862, his teammates of the Excelsior Club from South Brooklyn erected an impressive monument at Brooklyn's Green-Wood Cemetery in his memory. The granite obelisk incorporated a baseball motif, including bats, balls, and a score book, in its ornate design. For years, players and fans would make the pilgrimage to the cemetery to view Creighton's monument and pay their respects. In 1866, his former teammates and players from the National Club of Washington, D.C., accompanied Hall of Famer Henry Chadwick to visit his grave and pay tribute to the young man who was considered at that time the greatest ballplayer ever known. Some players were so moved that they went so far as cutting grass from his grave site for souvenirs. The Creighton monument served as the standard for future memorials to the greats of the game. (Courtesy of the National Baseball Hall of Fame Library, Cooperstown, New York.)

BASEBALL LEGENDS OF BROOKLYN'S GREEN-WOOD CEMETERY

Peter J. Nash

ARCADIA
PUBLISHING

Copyright © 2003 by Peter J. Nash
ISBN 978-1-5316-2013-4

Published by Arcadia Publishing
Charleston, South Carolina

Library of Congress Catalog Card Number: 2003111662

For all general information contact Arcadia Publishing at:
Telephone 843-853-2070
Fax 843-853-0044
E-mail sales@arcadiapublishing.com
For customer service and orders:
Toll-Free 1-888-313-2665

Visit us on the Internet at www.arcadiapublishing.com

Dedicated to my father and the late Frank "Chick" Keegan, two Brooklyn legends.

Green-Wood Cemetery was established on land over which the first Revolutionary War skirmishes of the Battle of Brooklyn were fought in 1776. Later, in the 19th century, the dignified Gothic Revival gates of Green-Wood, located at the base of Brooklyn's Gowanus Hills, witnessed the funeral processions of many prominent figures in American history, including Samuel F.B. Morse, Horace Greeley, and DeWitt Clinton, as well as household names such as Tiffany, Steinway, and Currier and Ives. (Clinton's bronze monument appears above.) The gates have also witnessed the likes of infamous mobster Albert Anastasia and the corrupt politician "Boss Tweed" of New York's Tammany Hall. But to the baseball fan, most relevant is the fact that close to 200 players and officials who pioneered our national game of baseball have also passed through these gates.

CONTENTS

Acknowledgments   6

Introduction   7

1.   The Fathers of Baseball   13

2.   The Original Knickerbockers   23

3.   The Gothams, Eagles, and Putnams   35

4.   The Baseball Conventions   47

5.   The Excelsiors and the Great Rebellion   63

6.   The Mighty Atlantics   79

7.   Baseball's First Professionals   93

8.   The Business of Baseball   99

9.   Ballparks, "Bums," and Beyond   113

ACKNOWLEDGMENTS

This work is the culmination of years of research, and I would like to recognize all of the individuals who assisted so generously in its production. Documenting Green-Wood's links to baseball's history would not have been possible without the support of Richard J. Moylan (Green-Wood's president) and his genuine interest in the preservation of the cemetery's rich history and ongoing efforts to make sure it has relevance in the future. His staff was instrumental in assisting with the project. I thank Ken Taylor (vice president), Nicholas Vislocky (superintendent), and Eugene Adamo for providing access to the grounds; Theresa LaBianca for verifying identities through cemetery records; and Louis LaBianca, James Loiacono, Richard Sneddon, Carmine Trunzo, Mario LaMalfa, and Jerry Martucci for their help in locating elusive players in unmarked lots. In addition, Brooklynite Vince Katinas offered his expertise on Green-Wood and Brooklyn's founding families. Special thanks go to cemetery historian Jeffrey Richman for his generous contribution of photographs from his personal collection and his unbridled enthusiasm for uncovering Green-Wood's "buried treasure." I also appreciate his contributions in helping to edit the book.

I also thank the National Baseball Hall of Fame Library in Cooperstown, including Jim Gates, Tim Wiles, Tom Sheiber, Bill Francis, Pat Kelly, and William C. Burdick for their invaluable research assistance.

My gratitude goes out to the Adams, Chadwick, Curry, Dunn, Mazolla, Reiferson, Russo, Pidgeon, Pinto, Polhemus, and Van Cott families, as well as David Block and Andrew Schiff, for providing valuable information and rare images that were instrumental in documenting Green-Wood's unique connection to baseball.

As an alumnus of Bishop Ford High School, I hope that this book will provide Frank Fusco and the school's baseball club with a new tool to teach the history of the early game in Brooklyn.

I thank Arcadia Publishing's Tiffany Howe for her enthusiasm and her decision to pursue such an unusual subject, and I thank my beautiful wife, Roxanne, both for her support and for putting up with the mess of my research paperwork, as well as my many trips back to Brooklyn.

Lastly, I would like to thank all of the individuals and organizations assisting me in the development of the Elysian Fields Monument Trust—a vehicle by which actual monuments and headstones can be installed at the now unmarked grave sites of so many baseball legends. The trust will work towards the day when every baseball legend at Green-Wood lies beneath a monument commemorating his life.

I am indebted to Green-Wood's first baseball historians, Henry Chadwick and Charles Peverelly, for their pioneer works, *The American Game of Baseball* (1868) and *The American Book of Pastimes* (1866), respectively. Chadwick and his rival Will Rankin also provided a wealth of useful information within their voluminous scrapbooks and other collected materials. Important additional source materials include the following: DeClerico and Pavelec's *The Jersey Game*, 1991; Frank Graham's *The Brooklyn Dodgers*, 1947; Elijah Kennedy's *John B. Woodward*, 1897; Harold Peterson's *The Man Who Invented Baseball*, 1973; Jim Reisler's *Babe Ruth Slept Here*, 1999; Jeffrey Richman's *Brooklyn's Green-Wood Cemetery*, 1998; Alfred Spink's *The National Game*, 1911; Jerry Malloy's rerelease of *Sol White's History of Colored Base Ball*, 1995; and the Society for American Baseball Research's *Nineteenth Century Stars*, 1989, and *Baseball's First Stars*, 1996.

INTRODUCTION

In antiquity, man first embraced the concept of Elysium; the feeling of euphoria experienced by the blessed after death. It was believed that once they had passed on, warriors were welcomed into a netherworld of plush grasslands known as the Elysian Fields. Centuries later, in antebellum New York, young men fashioned a pastoral playground of their own across the Hudson River in Hoboken, New Jersey, and appropriately named their retreat the Elysian Fields. However, the men who roamed these grasslands were living merchants and brokers in straw hats who were particularly interested in a new pastime called "base ball," and as they played on the fields of Hoboken, the growing interest in open-air recreation for the improvement of one's health gave new meaning to the concept of Elysium.

Upon the Elysian Fields, these 19th-century men competed and formed clubs of their own, establishing what came to be known as the national pastime. Americans were looking beyond the English tradition of cricket for their own sporting identity, and these social organizations known as the Knickerbocker, Gotham, and Eagle Clubs began to expose this new sport to ladies and gentlemen alike who retreated to Hoboken to escape the hustle and bustle of the growing metropolis. In the years from 1845 through the late 1860s, they witnessed many of these men engage in historic baseball contests that captivated the nation and carried the game to every corner of the country.

But, as the game grew, the once pristine Elysian Fields were cut up into lots for residences, railroads, and industry. By 1870, the game had produced its first generation of old-timers, and with each passing year, they faded from public view as new players embraced a game that had become a purely professional endeavor. As the pioneer baseball scribe Henry Chadwick noted, the game had undergone a natural evolution as it passed from a simple gentleman's game to a robust capitalistic enterprise. In the passing years, the game's true pioneers were all but forgotten.

Some, like veteran G. Stanton Smith of Brooklyn's Resolute Club, endeavored to keep their memory alive, writing the following to the *Brooklyn Daily Eagle* in 1895 to reminisce about his fellow old-timers:

> The great national game is indebted to these old veterans in more ways than one. In the first place there was no salary; on the contrary, there was an initiation fee and all had to pay dues and furnish their own uniforms, and pay their own travel expenses. The consequence was the different businesses they followed were neglected, and, with few exceptions, they accumulated little of this world's goods. [Their] crooked fingers test[ed] many a hot grounder and difficult fly . . . I know of no more deserving ones than the few who are of those old veterans, who back in the fifties, sacrificed their business futures, disfigured themselves for life, while contributing their efforts to make popular the 'national game' of America today.

Smith's words painted a vivid picture of the old timers' dedication to a game that eventually grew in scope far beyond their wildest imaginations. These men built the game from the ground up, but, as they left the field, they vanished into virtual obscurity. As their Elysian Fields became a distant memory, many of these same men soon disappeared to a common resting place for their collective crooked fingers and broken bones, Brooklyn's Green-Wood Cemetery. There they rest in peace amidst the rural tranquility and rolling green hillsides of what became, along with Niagara Falls, a premier tourist attraction of 19th-century America. By the time the National Baseball Hall of Fame was opened in 1939 in Cooperstown, New York, the exploits of these trailblazers had taken a backseat to the myth of Gen. Abner Doubleday's supposed invention of the game. Little did anyone realize, at the time, that the early history of the great

American pastime had already found a home at Green-Wood.

I was first introduced to Green-Wood by my freshman English teacher, Ralph Simonetti, at Brooklyn's Bishop Ford High School, which borders the cemetery. As a young member of the Society for American Baseball Research in 1982, I read an article Bill Ivory had written on the burial sites of Hall of Famers, and, after corresponding with him, I sent him a photograph I had taken of Henry Chadwick's Green-Wood monument. It sparked my interest in the 19th-century game, and I soon discovered that other baseball figures were buried at Green-Wood as well, including Jim Creighton and Dodger patriarch Charles Ebbets. Long before the cemetery had compiled databases of burial information, I regularly began searching for other players, and, years later, by sheer chance I stumbled upon a weathered white marble monument that literally stopped me in my tracks. It read, "Duncan Curry. Father of Baseball." Not only was Green-Wood home to "Father" Chadwick, but now a competing claim for baseball's paternal rights surfaced in the form of the original Knickerbocker Club president.

With the discovery of the Curry monument, I began to search in earnest and photograph other baseball monuments. Much to my amazement, this research yielded remarkable results. Green-Wood, the most prominent of all historic American cemeteries, was a well-preserved baseball time capsule. Arlington National Cemetery is home to our country's fallen military heroes, but nearly all of the important baseball heroes of the 19th century found their final rest amongst the half million or so men and women who now inhabit Green-Wood. The majority of the Knickerbocker, Atlantic, Putnam, and Excelsior Clubs are all here. Ballplayers, Civil War veterans, magnates, and misfits alike all contribute to what has become a living history of 19th-century baseball in the land of the dead.

Some are buried in unmarked graves in their original club uniforms, while others are honored with fitting monuments erected in their memory. These memorials, in most cases, are the players' only tangible link to the present. Luckily, time has not obliterated many of the surviving photographs and engravings of these legends, and the incorporation of the rare images within this work helps connect actual faces with the names etched on tombstones.

Hall of Famer Chadwick first recognized Green-Wood's significance to the game as he attended the funerals of so many fallen players and former colleagues there. In the end, like those who had passed before him, it was important to Chadwick that his last stop on earth was Green-Wood.

After visiting Henry Chadwick's grave on the anniversary of his death for decades, Ebbets continued a Brooklyn baseball tradition when he, too, was interred at Green-Wood.

Organized baseball first came to prominence in the 1840s and 1850s in the vicinities of New York City and across the Hudson River in Hoboken. It was upon Hoboken's Elysian Fields that pioneer ball clubs like the Knickerbockers and Gothams established the "New York Game;" however, it was upon the plush fields of Green-Wood Cemetery that the mortal remains of these veteran ballplayers were reunited. At Green-Wood, they reside among an illustrious group of men and women in what original cemetery planners likened to a necropolis: a city of the dead. By the time many of these men were interred at Green-Wood, the cemetery had become one of the foremost tourist attractions of the Victorian age. Stereoview images such as the one seen above were popular in the 1860s and 1870s.

Memorials at Green-Wood Cemetery served as models for future tributes to the game's greats, including Yankee Stadium's Monument Park, which features large stones dedicated to Hall of Famers Babe Ruth, Lou Gehrig, Joe DiMaggio, and Mickey Mantle. (Courtesy of the National Baseball Hall of Fame Library, Cooperstown, New York.)

9

Henry Chadwick is Green-Wood's only member of the National Baseball Hall of Fame, having been elected posthumously in 1938. However, long before that, he was honored in 1865 in *Frank Leslie's Illustrated Newspaper* in a steel engraving that featured the premier baseball men of the day. Green-Wood figured prominently in the rendering, its focal point being a shrouded image of baseball's martyr, James Creighton Jr., surrounded by his future Green-Wood neighbors: Thomas Dakin, Dr. William H. Bell, Robert Manly, James Whyte Davis, Thomas Van Cott, Thomas Miller, John Wildey, and Thomas G. Voorhies. The central image features a match between the Atlantics and Eckfords at Brooklyn's Union Grounds, owned and operated by William Cammeyer, another Green-Wood resident. Within months, some of the players featured made their pilgrimage to the Creighton monument. Today, Creighton and the game's pioneers are all but forgotten, having never received their due in Cooperstown. However, strong arguments can be made that Creighton, Duncan Curry, William Wheaton, James Whyte Davis, Thomas Dakin, William Van Cott, Thomas Van Cott, Charles Smith, John C. Chapman, Asa Brainard, and William Cammeyer are all worthy of enshrinement in the Baseball Hall of Fame.

HENRY CHADWICK—"Father of Base Ball."

Henry Chadwick was considered by many as the "Father of Baseball" in recognition of his tireless promotion of the game during the 19th century. He theorized that the game had evolved from the English game of rounders and played a key role in establishing it as the national pastime. He revolutionized baseball journalism, fought gambling and corruption, promoted the game in newspapers and manuals, perfected the box score, invented the method for scoring games, introduced statistical analysis, and, thus, invented what we now know as the modern-day batting average.

When Chadwick died on April 20, 1908, baseball luminaries paid their last respects and sent elaborate floral arrangements to the funeral, one of which, sent by Philadelphia A's manager Connie Mack, spelled out "Good Night." Chadwick's pallbearers included Harry Pulliam, National League president, and Brooklyn's Charles Ebbets. Green-Wood Cemetery was well attended by baseball figures such as old Atlantic John C. Chapman, sporting-goods king Andrew Peck, and future Hall of Famer John Ward. For years, Ebbets and *Brooklyn Daily Eagle* newspaperman Abe Yager visited Chadwick's grave on the anniversary of his death.

One

THE FATHERS OF BASEBALL

Green-Wood Cemetery was the brainchild of Brooklyn resident Henry Pierrepont and was incorporated in 1838 as the first rural cemetery in the New York metropolitan vicinity. As the cemetery grew, so, too, did the public's interest in the new game of baseball. By 1863, famed church architect Richard Upjohn built the Gothic Revival gates of the cemetery pictured above, and baseball was well on its way to establishing itself as the national pastime. In later years, Green-Wood served as the final resting place for scores of ballplayers and officials who helped establish the game in its infancy. Long before the invention of the Abner Doubleday myth and the establishment of the National Baseball Hall of Fame and Museum in Cooperstown, New York, Green-Wood served as a hidden baseball shrine of sorts for the game's true pioneers and architects, who, over the years, unfortunately became baseball's forgotten heroes.

Henry Chadwick was long employed by sporting-goods king and magnate Albert G. Spalding as the editor of his annual baseball guides. Spalding once promised Chadwick that he would purchase him a plot at Green-Wood and one day erect a monument over his grave. In the winter of 1905, just days after attending his own sister's funeral only a few yards away from the monument of Jim Creighton, Chadwick had an attorney draft his last will and testament, which specified Spalding's promises.

Spalding ultimately made good on his word, as he had already purchased a lot for Chadwick at Green-Wood, but he enlisted the help of Brooklyn Dodgers owner Charles Ebbets and scorecard and hot dog king Harry M. Stevens to help raise funds for a suitable monument by subscription to the National League.

HARRY STEVENS STARTS CHADWICK MEMORIAL

Noted Score Card Man Subscribes $100 to Fund for a Monument.

REMINDER FOR SPALDING IN CHADWICK'S WILL.

The will of Henry Chadwick, the "Father of Baseball," was filed in the Surrogate's Office to-day. His real estate is valued at $500, and his personal property at $500. He bequeaths everything to his wife, Jane Chadwick. Albert G. Spalding and William C. Edwards are named as executors. In his will Mr. Chadwick wrote: "I remind Albert G. Spalding of his promise to me that a monument shall be erected over my grave in Greenwood Cemetery."

Charles Ebbets and his associates chose a local monument sculptor named Grant Pitbladdo to execute a monument for Chadwick designed by sportswriter Francis Richter's daughter, Florence. The *Spalding League Guide* stated, "It will not be too ornate, showy or ostentatious, but a simple and solid affair in keeping with the life of the man whose virtues it marks."

Grant Pitbladdo and his Brooklyn Monument Company cleverly incorporated bronze replicas of bats, a glove, and a catcher's mask along with a bronze plaque in the shape of a baseball diamond that read, "In Memoriam, Henry Chadwick, Father of Base Ball." Over the years, the bronze has oxidized and turned a pale shade of green.

The Chadwick Monument was to be unveiled on the first anniversary of his death on April 20, 1909, but weather conditions proved too treacherous for the 90-year-old Jane Chadwick and others who gathered to pay homage to the deceased. Instead, the ceremony took place the next day and, after a prayer by Rev. Dr. T.E. Potterton, Lenora V. Caylor, daughter of the late sportswriter O.P. Caylor, pulled a cord that removed a draped American flag and unveiled the monument. The National League provided beds of pansies, roses, evergreen, and holly to adorn the monument year-round, while sculptor Pitbladdo crafted four granite bases with realistic straps that formed a baseball diamond around the grave. The monument was topped by a massive baseball of carved granite with a subtly sculpted figure eight baseball stitch. William Hudson of the *Brooklyn Daily Eagle* delivered an oration, and Charles Ebbets, on behalf of the National and American Leagues, formally presented the monument to Chadwick's widow.

Above is the Chadwick monument as it looks today. Nearing its 100th birthday, it has served as a popular tourist attraction at Green-Wood Cemetery and is a must-see destination for any authentic baseball road trip. In tribute to the game's symbolic father, fans often leave American flags at the base of his grave, and some even leave baseballs.

Although Chadwick was looked upon by many as the "Father of Baseball," he never considered himself that and stated frequently that, "Baseball, like Topsy, never had no fodder, it just growed up." Nonetheless, he still reveled in his status as the game's symbolic patriarch, and that caused some other writers, like the envious Will Rankin, to criticize and belittle Chadwick as he was growing both elderly and sickly. Chadwick, however, had the last laugh. His Green-Wood monument paved his way towards baseball immortality.

To counter Chadwick's evolutionary theory of baseball's English origin, his friend and employer, Albert Spalding, formed a special investigative commission to settle the dispute. However, it was nothing short of a sham, as Spalding directed the commission to prove baseball was only of American origin. An elderly Denver miner named Abner Graves provided testimony indicating that Gen. Abner Doubleday, pictured on the right, invented baseball in Cooperstown c. 1839, and thus, Spalding had the means by which to establish the Doubleday myth.

Chadwick strongly disagreed with Spalding, as did fellow writer Will Rankin, who was outraged with what he referred to as Spalding's "fake story." The commission published its findings in the 1908 *Spalding League Guide* just a month before Chadwick's death, and soon after, his rival Rankin wrote a rebuttal on the pages of the *Sporting News*, proclaiming that Alexander Cartwright, an original Knickerbocker, was the true "Father of Baseball."

In the course of Spalding's investigation, Rankin recalled his conversations with Knickerbocker player Duncan Curry, the club's first president. While chatting with Curry and ex-player Robert Ferguson, Curry supposedly exclaimed, "Thomas Fiddlesticks. [Chadwick] had no more to do with the original rules than you had. William Wheaton, William H. Tucker and I drew up the first set of rules and the game was developed by the people who played it and were connected with it." Nowhere did Curry ever mention Alexander Cartwright's involvement. Charles Peverelly was the first to mention Cartwright's role as a pioneer in his 1866 *Book of American Pastimes*. Judge William Van Cott, pioneer of the Gotham Club, also recalled how Cartwright took his plans to the baseball field and was ridiculed. Nonetheless, a case can be made that Curry, Wheaton, Tucker, and Cartwright were the true founding fathers of the modern game.

After serving as Knickerbocker president from 1845 to 1846, Duncan Curry remained a prominent club member and player for many years. In 1853, he was assigned to a committee for rules comprised of his teammates William Tucker and "Doc" Adams, as well as members of the Eagle Club. Cartwright went west in the gold rush and severed ties to the Knicks, while Curry remained an active member. Upon his death and burial in 1894, his Green-Wood monument proclaimed that he was the father of baseball and the "First President of the Knickerbocker Base Ball Club, the First Ball Club Ever Organized." For well over a century, the inscription on the Curry monument eluded mention in Brooklyn newspapers and the national baseball press.

With four men vying for the title of "Father of Baseball," it is fitting that all of them have found a common resting place at Green-Wood Cemetery. Baseball's development was an evolutionary process, and each of these men played a part in the establishment and improvement of what ultimately became the national pastime. But even today, most still believe that Gen. Abner Doubleday invented the game. Spalding, in a stroke of marketing genius, created the fiction that Americans yearned for: a creation myth that tied the birth of the national game to the supposed ingenuity of an American war hero. Before Spalding solidified his scheme, however, he provided the ultimate irony at Chadwick's 1908 funeral, as he sent a large ball of white immortelles accentuated with purple ribbon creating the stitch of a baseball, with red flowers spelling out the words "The Father of Base Ball." In the distance is Green-Wood's bare Battle Hill long before it was transformed with headstones and monuments.

Two

THE ORIGINAL
KNICKERBOCKERS

Baseball first planted its roots upon the Elysian Fields of Hoboken with the Knickerbocker Club of New York serving as the game's pioneer organization. They formulated the style of play known as the "New York Game" and adhered to the principles of play that fostered both social interaction and healthful recreation. The Knicks were comprised of men from prominent New York families who worked as bankers, physicians, brokers, photographers, lawyers, and firefighters. Long after their careers on the field had ended, the majority of the club's members were reunited in Brooklyn within the confines of the rural scenery of Green-Wood Cemetery. As Green-Wood historian Jeffrey Richman has noted, "Everyone who was anybody in nineteenth century New York wanted to be buried there, and they were." The Knickerbocker ballplayers who served as captains of industry and sporting mavericks were of like mind, as their many funereal monuments are scattered about the serene cemetery grounds. In 1865, Alexander Cartwright wrote to future Green-Wood resident Charles De Bost, "Dear old Knickerbockers I hope that the club is still kept up, and that I shall someday meet again with them on the pleasant fields of Hoboken."

The Knicks played on a plot at New York City's 27th Street in 1842 and moved to Murray Hill near Third Avenue in 1844. The next year, they formally organized, drafting bylaws and rules of play as they moved to Hoboken's Elysian Fields, and, on June 19, 1846, they played their first match against an opposing team known as the New York Club. By the late 1850s, the club was no longer battling other clubs in Brooklyn, such as the Excelsior, Atlantic, and Putnam Clubs, who would soon overshadow the once-mighty Knickerbockers. The panoramic image depicted above by Brooklyn photographer Charles H. Williamson (also buried in

Green-Wood) shows both the Knick and Excelsior Clubs posing in 1859 for what is considered to be the first photograph ever taken on a ball field. The image captures perhaps the only known photographs of some players now interred at Green-Wood: James Whyte Davis (second from the left), Charles De Bost (third from the left), Dr. J.B. Jones (in an overcoat and a hat), Henry D. Polhemus (to the right of Jones), John Holder (sixth from the right), Edwin Russell (fifth from the right), and Thomas Reynolds (far right).

James Whyte Davis began his baseball career with the New York Club in 1845. By 1850, he had been elected as a member of the Knickerbockers. He was elected president of the club in 1858, 1859, and 1860. He is credited for writing baseball's first song in 1854 entitled "Ball Days." His 1858 version of the song debuted at a postgame banquet with Brooklyn's Excelsior Club and, appropriately, Davis paid tribute to many of the ballplayers who now join him at Green-Wood: "the witty Doctor Jones," Gus Dayton, and John Holder of the Excelsiors, Thomas Dakin of the Putnams whom he called "a trump," Thomas Van Cott and Louis Wadsworth of the Gothams, Thomas Miller of the Empire Club, and his teammate Charles De Bost.

Wrapped in the Original Flag
of the
Knickerbocker Base Ball Club of N. Y.,
Here lies the body of
James Whyte Davis,
A member for thirty years.
He was not "Too Late,"
Reaching the "Home Plate."
Born March 2, 1826.
Died———————

In 1893, an elderly James Whyte Davis wrote to sportswriter Joe Vila stating that, upon his death, he wanted to be buried in his Knickerbocker uniform and wrapped in the original team flag, which he still retained. He also suggested that 10¢ be collected from all players and officials of the National League to erect a suitable monument to his memory. A retort was sent to Vila by a "young Knickerbocker" who disputed Davis's claim to being the eldest Knick and voiced his support for Duncan Curry as the true father of baseball.

James Whyte Davis's dreams of baseball immortality fell far short and, sadly, the legendary baseball figure and pioneer Knickerbocker was unceremoniously buried at Green-Wood on a blustery February day in 1899. But, as he requested, Davis was dressed in his Knickerbocker best and wrapped in the team flag he so cherished. For the last century, he has passed the days in the unmarked grave pictured above. When his plot was photographed for this work, all that adorned his grave was a tattered fragment of an American flag.

BASE BALL PLAY.—The subjoined is the result of the return match between the New York Base Ball Club and the Brooklyn players, which came off on the ground of the Brooklyn Star Cricket Club yesterday. Messrs. Johnson, Wheaton and Van Nostrand were the umpires.

NEW YORK BALL CLUB.		BROOKLYN CLUB.	
Hands out.	Runs.	Hands out.	Runs.
Davis,..... 2	4	Hunt...... 1	3
Murphy... 0	6	Hines,...... 2	2
Vail....... 2	4	Gilmore.... 3	2
Kline.,.... 1	4	Hardy...... 2	2
Miller..... 2	5	Sharp....... 2	2
Case...... 2	4	Meyers..... 0	3
Tucker.... 2	4	Whaley..... 2	2
Winslow... 1	6	Forman..... 1	3
12	37	12	19

This box score appeared in the *New York Herald* on October 23, 1845, and recorded the outcome of one of the earliest matches ever played between the New York and Brooklyn Clubs. James Whyte Davis excelled for the victorious New Yorkers scoring 4 of their 37 runs. The game was umpired by another Green-Wood alumnus, William Wheaton. Having played such an integral part in codifying the original set of Knickerbocker rules, Wheaton was often called to duty as the arbiter of matches and, thus, became one of baseball's first umpires.

James Whyte Davis (right) is shown as he appeared in 1859, dressed in his Knickerbocker uniform, which included pants, a belt, a hat, and a shirt. The Knicks were the first club to introduce uniforms to the game in 1849. By the time Davis posed for this shot, the Knicks abandoned straw caps for the mohair type held by Davis in this image. (Courtesy of the National Baseball Hall of Fame Library, Cooperstown, New York.)

Fraley Niebuhr was a close friend of Alexander Cartwright and an original Knickerbocker who worked as a clerk at the U.S. Custom House in New York. He made the club's historic first trip to Hoboken in 1845 and scored three runs for Duncan Curry's victorious team in the first intrasquad game on October 6 versus Cartwright's side. Niebuhr was one of the most skilled Knick players and also served as the club secretary in 1848 and 1849. He was elected vice president in 1850, and, by 1853, he was voted club president and retained that position until he was replaced in 1855, when he became a club director.

William Wheaton, a New York City attorney, was vice president of the Knickerbockers in 1845 and, along with Cartwright and Curry, played a significant role in drafting the game's first formal set of rules, which were adopted on September 23, 1845. Both Wheaton and his roommate, William H. Tucker (another Green-Wood resident), served together as the Knickerbocker Committee on By-Laws and affixed their signatures to the final draft of the 1845 bylaws, which included the playing rules.

The formalization of the Knickerbocker rules took place at the Barclay Street establishment of a friend of the club named Fijux. Aptly known as Fijux's Hotel, its proprietor hosted many Knick team gatherings thereafter. Fijux's young son was named baseball's first mascot at a club dinner. The club's minute books stated, "The young fellow was duly brought forward and received a kiss from all present. He was then placed in the center of the table and duly christened Charles Knickerbocker Fijux and the Secretary directed to place his name on the Roll." Pictured is the Fijux family monument, the last resting place of baseball's first team mascot.

John Paulding debuted in the Knickerbocker lineup on April 10, 1846, and played for the club in its famous June 19, 1846, match versus the New York Club. That event marked the first match the Knicks ever played against another competing club, but it was a forgettable one for the Knickerbockers, who lost by an embarrassing score of 23-1. It is believed that Paulding was related by marriage to author Washington Irving, who may have provided the inspiration to name the club after his beloved Deitrich Knickerbocker character.

Commercial merchant Daniel Tryon played for the Knicks in the famous 1846 match versus New York and continued to play throughout the 1850s. He played an integral part in the Knickerbocker victories over the Gothams in 1853 and 1854, but, by 1861, he met an early death. His teammate Henry Titus Morgan made a living as a Wall Street broker and joined the Knicks in 1845. He accompanied his 28 teammates across the Hudson to play their first intrasquad matches but did not actually make his playing debut until the club's fifth intrasquad game, on October 17, 1845.

Knickerbocker Alonzo Slote belonged to the firm of Tredwell & Slote and augmented his commercial success with civic duty in New York City's volunteer fire department. He served the Oceana Hose Company No. 36 valiantly as their fire captain with his Knickerbocker teammate William Woodhull, who later became a fire department president. Their ball playing careers spanned through the 1850s, as they also played for baseball clubs representing their respective fire companies.

Alonzo Slote was elected Knickerbocker vice president for the seasons of 1862 and 1863. His brother, Henry, was also a Knick member in good standing and served as their official scorer on many occasions. In 1854, he founded the stationery firm of Slote and Janes at 140 Nassau Street and frequently supplied the club with their letterheads and club score books. Both brothers are now buried in Green-Wood, though Alonzo has the more prominent monument pictured here.

A shining example of the Knickerbockers' gentlemanly code was the career of James Wenman, who played shortstop in the 1850s. Wenman embarked on a career as a firefighter that encompassed decades of heroic service for the citizens of New York. He played baseball for the Knicks in his leisure time but was also named foreman of the fire department. In 1859, he retired and assumed the position as the Knickerbocker Club's secretary.

James Wenman was also a formidable figure in the financial markets as a cotton broker. He was a great patron of both the Metropolitan Museum of Art and the American Museum of Natural History. After serving on the art museum's board of trustees, he was elected as an honorary Fellow for Life, and, in 1876, he was appointed by Mayor Wickham as a commissioner of Central Park. His humble grave is adorned by a granite slab devoid of any inscription or identification of this famous Knickerbocker and his stellar firefighting and baseball careers.

William Vail was one of the original men to play in 1844 on New York City's Murray Hill. He was nicknamed "Stay-where-you-am-Wail" and starred for the New York Club in the historic 1845 match versus Brooklyn and the June 19, 1846, match versus the Knickerbockers. In 1852, he joined the upstart Knickerbocker rivals the Gotham Club and remained their star player until 1857, when he disappeared from the baseball scene. His family plot and unmarked grave are pictured here.

The Knickerbockers' first matches were amongst themselves and were never recorded on paper, but, by October 6, 1845, the club had established its own official score book. One of the new faces in the lineup that day was that of Archibald Gourlie, a Wall Street broker who batted last in the order on president Duncan Curry's side. The score book reveals that Gourlie was fined six pence for protesting an umpire's call, thus becoming the first player ever penalized on the ball field. Long after his Knick career was over, he met his final rest at Green-Wood in the plot pictured above.

Charles Schuyler De Bost (left) was elected to the Knickerbocker Club in the late 1840s and first donned his uniform as its trusty backstop. Charles Peverelly remembered De Bost as, "very active and full of good humor, always creating much amusement upon the ball field; as a catcher he held the first rank for many years, and it may be asserted that he has never had a superior in that position." De Bost was a formidable batsman with considerable power, but as the writers of the day commented, he was "often put out, from a tendency to raise the ball." In his song "Ball Days," James Whyte Davis wrote how De Bost "shines out like a star."

At the apex of his career, De Bost appeared in the Fashion Race Course matches of 1858 as a catcher and captain for the New York all-stars. In the first contest, De Bost was reported to have been "lamed" when he was struck with a ball, but the warrior continued to play through the pain "with indomitable pluck and spirit." Above, he appears in an 1859 pose, hat in hand, as one of the game's first all-stars. The epitaph on his grave befits a ballplayer: "The strife is over, the battle done, the victory of life is won."

Three

THE GOTHAMS, EAGLES, AND PUTNAMS

This woodcut entitled *Base Ball in America* appeared on the cover of *Porter's Spirit of the Times* on September 12, 1857, and is the first-ever depiction in the press of an actual baseball game in progress. The appearance of the engraving was a testament to the game's growing popularity among what the paper referred to as "Young New York . . . the aspiring man of muscle, whose mind will make its mark all the more legible—because hardened by exercise, and thereby rendered fit for the battle of life." The game featured was dubbed a "great match at the Elysian Fields" between the Eagle and Gotham Clubs of New York and, as *Porter's Spirit of the Times* reported, a "splendid collection of feminine and juvenile beauty" witnessed the game. The Gothams experienced an uncharacteristic loss at the hands of the Eagles, who proved too much for the likes of Gotham players Louis F. Wadsworth, William Van Cott, Seamen Lichtenstein, and James Vail (all interred at Green-Wood). Gotham star-pitcher Thomas Van Cott sat out that day, missing his only game since the team's formation in 1852.

While most historians consider James Creighton the game's first great pitcher, the honor should actually go to Thomas Van Cott of the Gotham Club. Van Cott was nothing short of dominant in his pitching, putting together an unprecedented streak of victories for the Gothams. He was also their leading batsman, but he solidified his reputation with his pitching prowess. *Porter's Spirit of the Times* reported that he stood "very high as a pitcher, combining speed with an even ball."

William Van Cott was the founder and first president of the Gotham Club and an early veteran of the national game. He began his career playing with the Washington Club of New York City and, soon after, used his organizational skills to found a club centered on his talented brother Thomas. Van Cott sensed the potential of the fledgling game, as he predicted, in the 1854 *Porter's Spirit of the Times*, "Indications are that this noble game will, the coming season, assume a higher position as ever."

The Van Cott family plot at Green-Wood is located directly across from the elaborate and famous monument dedicated to young Charlotte Canda, pictured here, which was a very popular 19th-century tourist attraction. But like so many forgotten baseball legends, the trio of William, Gabriel, and Thomas lie in unmarked graves. A monument honoring the lives of this trio of baseball royalty is long overdue.

NEW YORK CLIPPER.

JULY 16, 1853.

| HARRISON TRENT, Proprietor. | FRANK QUEEN, Editor. |

July 16 **BASE BALL.** 1853

The first friendly game of the season, between the Gotham and Knickerbocker Base Ball Clubs was played on the grounds of the latter on the 5th inst. The game was commenced on Friday the 1st, but owing to the storm had to be postponed, the Knickerbockers making nine aces to two of the Gotham, the following is the score for both days:

GOTHAM.

	No of Outs.	Runs.
Vail	1	3
W. H. Fancott	2	2
Thos. Fancott	2	2
J. C. Pinkney	0	3
R. H. Cudlip	2	1
Winslow, Jr.	4	0
Winslow, Sr.	2	0
Jno. Lalor	2	1
Wadsworth	3	0
Total	18	12

KNICKERBOCKER.

Pictured here is a July 16, 1853, game account and box score of a famous Gotham-Knickerbocker battle printed by Frank Queen's *New York Clipper*. It was the newspaper's first published box score. Note how the Van Cott name is misspelled.

This rare image of the Gotham Club of 1856 has been rightfully dubbed by historian Tom Sheiber as the earliest baseball team photograph and features all three Van Cott brothers: Gabriel (sitting second from the right), Thomas (on the far left holding a ball) and William (seated on the left). The Gothams surpassed the Knickerbockers as the premier team in New York City, but for the most part, their success was due to the skillful pitching of Thomas. Left fielder Phil Sheridan (standing fifth from the left) and first baseman James Vail (standing third from the right) later joined their teammates as permanent Green-Wood residents. (Courtesy of the National Baseball Hall of Fame Library, Cooperstown, New York.)

This box score appeared on the front page of the *New York Daily Times* in 1855 reporting that the Gothams vanquished the Eagle Club 21-3. Gabriel Van Cott served as umpire. After the match, Van Cott and the rest of the Gotham Club entertained the Eagles with "a cold collation" in the newly established custom of the postgame banquet.

NEW-YORK, SATUR

...'s to which they are consigned in our growing City, and will ultimately, take a place among the most useful of the benevolent institutions for which New York is justly famed, and be an enluring monument to the energy, parental sympathy, and heaven-born charity of its founders."

Base Ball—Eagle vs. Gotham Club.

These clubs played a match yesterday at the Red House, Harlem, which resulted in favor of the Gotham. The game was very short and indifferently played—the Eagles only got 3 runs and the Gothams 21 in four innings, with two men to go out. They just got through in time to save the rain. After the play the Gotham Club entertained the Eagle Club and their friends with a cold collation. The following is the score.

EAGLE CLUB		GOTHAM CLUB.	
1 Hyatt	0	1 T. Van Cott	2
2 Smith	0	2 Burns	2
3 Gibbs	0	3 Sheridan	4
4 Connor	0	4 W. Van Cott	2
5 Place	1	5 Teed	4
6 Colgate	1	6 Case	4
7 Winterbottom	0	7 McFarlane	2
8 Baker	1	8 Cudlipp	0
9 Harrison	0	9 Vale	1
Total	3	Total	21

Runs—First innings.		Runs—First inning.	
Second	3	Second	7
Third	0	Third	4
Fourth	0	Fourth	4

Pitcher, Gibbs ; Behind, Place . Judge, Mott.   Pitcher, T. Van Cott . Behind, Vale ; Judge, G. Van Cott.

Referee—Dr. Adams, of the Knickerbocker.

The return match of the Gotham and Knickerbocker, and a match between the Putnam, of East Brooklyn, and Astoria Clubs will be played—time not fixed.

Philip Sheridan joined the Gotham Club in 1854 and quickly established himself as a talented batsman for their nine. Early box scores demonstrate his ability to score runs, but Sheridan was ultimately considered an umpire more so than a player. Sheridan died at the turn of the 20th century and was buried in an unmarked grave in a public lot on the fringes of Green-Wood Cemetery bordering 37th Street.

Louis F. Wadsworth originally played with the Knickerbocker Club through 1856 and was one of their mainstays until he joined the Gothams after a reported dispute with the pioneer club. *Porter's Spirit of the Times* reported claims that his friends stated he was, "the best first base man in any club, perfectly fearless—he will stop any ball that may come within reach."

Seamen Lichtenstein established his own produce house in 1844 and soon became one of the most successful vegetable and fruit men in the country. Like other successful Manhattan merchants, he sought the social interaction and physical exercise available in the ranks of the growing organizations of the day and joined the Gotham Club. He appeared sporadically in box scores that identified him only as "Seamen," and he also served as the club's trusty treasurer during the late 1850s.

Chadwick. The old club-banner was then given to Mr. Davis at his special request, and shortly afterwards the party broke up.

We append a copy of the score of the opening game of 1857 between the Eagle and Knickerbocker Clubs:

EAGLE.	R.	KNICKERBOCKER.	R.
Hauseman, f.	3	Stevens, p.	2
Yates, 1st b	2	Welling, c.	2
Brinckerhoff, f.	3	Stansbury, 2d b.	2
Williams, 2d b.	4	Dr. Adams, s s	2
Bixby, p.	4	McLaughlin, 3d b	2
Welling, s s.	2	Kissam, f.	1
Baker, f.	1	Grinnell, f.	1
Gelston, c.	3	Tucker, 1st b.	2
Place, 3d b.	3	Davis, f.	2
Total	25	Total	16

Eagle............................4   1   12   2   6—25
Knickerbocker...................0   3   2   7   4—16

Umpires, Dr. Anthony and T. W. Mott. Referee, Mr. Teed of Gotham Club. Time of game, 3h.

Samuel Yates and the Eagles were rivals of the pioneer Knickerbockers, but their leader, James Whyte Davis, paid tribute to Yates and all other members of the ball-playing fraternity in his song "Ball Days" in 1858. The following lines are from the song: "The Nestors and the parents in this our noble game, May repose on laurels gathered and on records of their fame; But all honor and all glory to their ever fostering hand, That is multiplying ball clubs in towns throughout the land."

Davis appears with Yates in the 1857 box score pictured above.

Samuel Yates began his career as a Knickerbocker and was later the star infielder of New York's Eagle Club, regularly leading his team in the categories of batting average and runs scored. He played an integral part in the club's rise to prominence and led the Eagles to a 25-16 victory over the Knickerbockers in 1857. By 1861, he was chosen to represent the New York all-star nine at first base in the famous Great Match for the Silver Ball at the Elysian Fields in Hoboken. Seen here is the Yates family monument at Green-Wood.

The Putnam Club of Brooklyn was organized by its first president, Samuel Godwin, who took the Van Cotts' lead when he enlisted the services of his brother Richard while his other brother Daniel played for the Young America Club. The Godwins were later reunited in Green-Wood, with three separate monuments located in different sections of the cemetery. Samuel's monument, pictured here, is a well-shaded striking terra-cotta colored granite.

This box score and report from 1855 shows a victorious Putnam Club outmatching the inferior Astoria Club 23-2. The reporter, most likely a representative from one of the teams, noted specifically that Putnam player "R. Godwin as catcher was much admired."

PUTNAM CLUB RECORD.

Base Ball.

PUTNAM VS. ASTORIA CLUB.

The return game with the above two clubs was played yesterday on the Putnam Ground, East Brooklyn, and resulted in favor of Putnam, 23 to 2—the greatest defeat of the season. We never saw better batting than the Putnam displayed for the time they have been organized, and the play of R. Godwin as catcher, was much admired. The Astoria have not improved vastly since we last saw them; next season they may come out better After the game they all returned to the Riding School, where they were liberally entertained by the Putnam's. The Knickerbocker, Gotham and Columbia street clubs were ably represented, and if the weather had not been so cold more ladies would have been on the ground.

PUTNAM CLUB.		ASTORIA CLUB.	
Hoyt	2	Valentine	1
Dakin	3	Ethridge	0
J. E. Davison, Jr.	3	Trowbridge	0
E. Burr	3	Edwards	0
Cesner	3	Barton	0
More	3	Paynter	1
R. J. Godwin	1	Lathrop	0
Morrell	2	Nash	0
Davidson	3	Baldwin	0
Total	23	Total	2

Pitcher—Dakin.
Catcher—R. T. Godwin.
Judge—F. Jackson.
Referee—W. H. Drummond, of the Knickerbocker.

Pitcher—Valentine.
Catcher—Edwards.
Judge—Edwards.

Richard T. Godwin one of the premier catchers of his day, handled the pitching of the talented Putnam ace, Thomas Dakin. Demonstrating Green-Wood's status as a Victorian who's who, Godwin is buried across from the pyramid-like tomb of ASPCA founder Henry Burgh, an early fan of baseball as healthy outdoor recreation.

Thomas Dakin was the premier all-around player in Brooklyn years before Jim Creighton entered the fray. His combination of skillful pitching and powerful batting made him the envy of all clubs. Dakin was born in Orange County, New York, in 1831 and moved to New York to be an office boy. While playing for the Putnams, he established the firm of Thomas S. Dakin & Company as commission agents. Dakin was called to service during the Civil War and became captain of the 13th regiment, Brooklyn, in 1862. After the war, he returned to Brooklyn and played briefly with the Excelsior Club, but he continued his military service, earning the rank of major general of militia. He was an accomplished marksman, president of the National Rifle Association, a democratic nominee for Congress, and a leading member of baseball's Standing Committee on Rules. The monument erected at Green-Wood in his memory was featured in tourist guides and popular photographic stereoviews of the era.

Putnam team captain Thomas Dakin's likeness appeared in many of Henry Chadwick's early baseball manuals, including the 1865 edition of *Frank Leslie's Illustrated Newspaper*. As a pitcher, Dakin was known as, "one who loses no time in the delivery of the ball," and Chadwick ranked him among Thomas Van Cott of the Gothams, Frank Pidgeon of the Eckfords, and Mattie O'Brien of the Atlantics as one of the premier strategic pitchers of the day. To the right is an 1870s portrait of the more portly yet impeccable general in full military garb.

General Dakin's other claim to baseball fame is attributed to his discovery of a young Brooklyn pitcher and future Hall of Famer named Arthur "Candy" Cummings in 1866. He told Henry Chadwick, "You ought to see one of our junior players pitch, Mr. Chadwick. He actually curves the ball as it passes his hand to the bat. I cannot bat his pitching at all." When Chadwick visited the Capitoline Grounds to see the youngster curve the ball, Cummings was pitching to his catcher Herbert Jewell, another baseball legend buried in Green-Wood Cemetery.

William Van Cott was a New York City judge and the first president of the Gotham Club. In late 1856, the Knickerbockers, on the advice of their president Dr. Daniel Adams, proposed the formation of a baseball convention for delegates from the growing number of clubs to meet and discuss the state of the game and the need to organize themselves in a more formal legislative body. The group looked to Judge Van Cott for leadership, and they elected him in 1858 as the first president of the newly formed National Association of Base Ball Players. (Courtesy of the National Baseball Hall of Fame Library, Cooperstown, New York.)

Four

THE BASEBALL CONVENTIONS

The first baseball convention was held early in 1857 at Smith's Hotel on the corner of Broadway and Broome Street in Manhattan. This photograph shows the bustling thoroughfare in the early 1860s. Three delegates from each prominent club were requested to appear in order to discuss the merits of Doc Adams's and the Knickerbockers' submission of a formal set of rules for match play. These men, many of whom are buried at Green-Wood, served as the Franklins, Jeffersons, and Madisons of the early game, establishing baseball's founding principles and guidelines. As the baseball conventions spread the gospel of baseball near and far, new clubs were formed with patriotic names such as the Hamiltons, Continentals, Washingtons, and Young Americas.

Thomas G. Voorhies served as president of the Empire Club, which first organized on October 23, 1854, with just 11 members, and, by 1857, had grown to more than 40. The club utilized Hoboken's Elysian Fields as their home grounds and, as their elected president, Voorhis conducted club business from his office at 682 Broadway. This woodcut portrait was printed in 1865, when Voorhies was elevated to the position of president of the National Association of Base Ball Players. Below, the monument of Thomas G. Voorhies is pictured.

John J. Bloomfield was another member of the Empire Club who served with Voorhis as a delegate at the first baseball conventions. He also served the Empires for years as their elected club treasurer.

EMPIRE BASE BALL CLUB.—Match between the Light and Heavy Weights, played on Saturday last, the 13th inst. Owing to bad fielding of the Light Weights in the first inning, the Heavy made a score of eight runs, but the rest of the game shows good play on the part of the Light Weights.

LIGHT WEIGHTS (145lbs. and under).			HEAVY WEIGHTS (over 145lbs).		
Names.	Positions.		Names.	Positions.	
Culyer	s. stop	2	Miller	2d base	2
Chalmers	3d base	2	Leavy	1st base	1
Thorn	pitcher	1	Leaming	field	1
Carleton	field	1	Wardell	catcher	1
Hoyt	field	1	Merwin	s. stop	2
Scott	catcher	1	Gough	3d base	2
Voorhis	s. stop	0	Fayne	pitcher	3
Spadone	field	3	Bloomfield	field	1
Haydock	1st base	0	Cameron	field	1
Tice	2d base	0	Loper	field	2
Fargis	field	0	Saunders	field	0
Murphy	field	0	McGrath	field	0
Total		11	Total		16

Umpire—L. F. Wadsworth, Gotham B. B. C.

Clubs often played odd intrasquad matches, and in 1857, the Empire Club engaged in a match between its heavyweight and lightweight members. Thomas Voorhies was lighter on his feet than his friend Bloomfield, who weighed in somewhere over 145 pounds. The heavyweights prevailed by a score of 16-11.

Theodore F. Jackson, a lawyer by trade, was a member of Brooklyn's Putnam Club and served as the secretary of the first baseball convention's Committee of Rules in 1857. His Green-Wood monument is a massive piece of granite sculpted into a shape reminiscent of the stones adorning Easter Island. Jackson commissioned New York's famed Tiffany Studios to design the monument in 1913, shortly before his death. It is a fitting homage to the man who was elected vice president of the National Association of Base Ball Players in 1859 and who served many years on the association's Committee of Rules. Long after his ball-playing days had passed, he was appointed as park commissioner by Brooklyn's Mayor Chapin and also served Brooklyn as the city's controller. He was a close friend and confidant of another Green-Wood legend, former New York City Mayor Seth Low, the only man elected mayor of both New York City and Brooklyn.

turn commences at the player who stands on the list next to the one who lost the third hand.

§ 14. No ace or base can be made on a foul strike.

§ 15. A runner cannot be put out in making one base, when a balk is made by the pitcher.

§ 16. But one base allowed if the ball, when struck, bounds out of the field.

§ 17. The ball shall weigh from 5½ to 6 ounces, and be from 2¾ to 3¼ inches in diameter.

ARTICLE V.—ALTERATION OF CONSTITU-TION OR BY-LAWS.

§ 1. Every alteration, amendment or addition to this Constitution and By-Laws shall be delivered in writing to the President, who shall publish the same to the Club; and at the next regular meeting ensuing it shall be considered and adopted, if two-thirds of the members present concur.

§ 2. A by-law may be temporarily suspended by a vote of two-thirds of members present, at a stated or special meeting.

JNO. W. MOTT, *President.*

W. W. ARMFIELD, *Vice-President.*

RHINELANDER, *Secretary.*

REVISED

CONSTITUTION, BY-LAWS

AND

RULES

OF THE

EAGLE BALL CLUB,

ADOPTED 1854.

ORGANIZED 1840.

BL-247.56

New-York:

OLIVER & BROTHER, STEAM JOB PRINTERS.

1854.

John W. Mott was president and founder of the mighty Eagle Club of New York. Their team constitution, which was formally adopted in 1854, interestingly proclaims that the club was first organized in 1840, predating the Knickerbocker and New York Clubs. (Courtesy of the National Baseball Hall of Fame Library, Cooperstown, New York.)

Mott served as a delegate to the original conventions along with his vice president, W.W. Armfield. For many years, the Eagle president and his trusty assistant have shared their final resting place at Green-Wood.

Dr. William H. Bell represented Williamsburg's Eckford Club at the early conventions of the National Association of Base Ball Players as early as 1860 and later joined New York's Eclectic Club in the mid-1860s. Henry Chadwick later remembered him for his "enthusiastic love for the game."

Dr. Bell was the leader of many clubs, and Chadwick proclaimed that, "The Henry Eckford and Eclectic Clubs owe their existence to his untiring industry." Dr. Bell appears in the illustration of the 1858 Eckford Club as their umpire, seated on the far left, and also in Frank Leslie's famous 1865 engraving above.

William V. Babcock organized the Atlantic Club in June 1855. He recruited a group of friends who played upon the "old pigeon grounds" of Prospect Park in the first Atlantic intrasquad matches. He represented the club at the early baseball association meetings and was later named president of the club in 1864 and 1865. As an old man, he commented on the modern game *c.* 1895: "There will be less money in baseball next year . . . There is not enough interest in it for people, and I believe that we will have to go back to the old system of playing in order to popularize it again."

William A. Brown of Williamsburg, Brooklyn, played for the Eckford Club in the 1850s as its catcher and represented the club at many of the early baseball conventions. A popular Brooklyn figure, Brown entered politics as a clerk for the fourth district court and was appointed fire commissioner in 1869.

CHARTER OAK.	H. L.	RUNS.	HAMILTON.	H. L.	RUNS.
Davidson, catcher	2	2	A. J. Dayton, pitcher	2	2
Sanford, pitcher	1	3	J. S. Dayton, second base	3	2
Alton, field	2	0	Cooper, catcher	2	3
Hubbard, first base	2	1	Hall, first base	2	3
Bosworth, second base	4	0	Hunter, third base	4	1
Tuttle, field	1	3	Donaldson, field	1	3
Cutter, third base	2	2	Elmendorf, field	2	3
Wood, field	1	2	Wilber, field	0	3
Total		13	Total		20

SYNOPSIS:

CHARTER OAK.		HAMILTON.	
First Innings	1	First Innings	0
Second "	1	Second "	5
Third "	0	Third "	8
Fourth "	5	Fourth "	4
Fifth "	6	Fifth "	3

But five innings were played, on account of the darkness.

The playing of A. J. Dayton and Cooper, on our side, was fine, the latter making two home runs. On the other side, the playing of Sandford was almost unequalled for alertness in catching, and grace in handling the bat. He made many beautiful points during the game. We play a match with the Nassau's in about a week, when we expect to achieve a splendid victory, as it has been admitted by several, that our playing is much quicker and finer than theirs, and they will be unable to withstand the pitching of A. J. Dayton. Yours, with esteem, HAMILTON.

Augustus J. Dayton was considered a pitching phenomenon when he began his career with Brooklyn's Hamilton Club. His teammates had great confidence when he was in the box, and after his performance against Brooklyn's Charter Oak Club in 1857, a Hamilton Club official predicted the worst for their next opponent: "Our playing is much quicker and finer than theirs, and they will be unable to withstand the pitching of A.J. Dayton."

Gus Dayton's services were so sought after that he set off one of the first baseball controversies regarding a player jumping from one club to another when the Excelsiors talked him into jumping to their club from the Hamiltons. As one of baseball's first free agents, Dayton ultimately left the Excelsiors to join the Pastime Club and then, finally, moved on to play for the Putnams. Years later, Dayton made his final jump to this modest plot at Green-Wood.

Robert Manly also appeared in the Green-Wood dominated Frank Leslie illustration in 1865 as an early standout for the Star of Brooklyn Club. He remained an avid player through the decades of the 1850s and 1860s, when the players slowly made the transition from amateur to professional status. By 1870, he was considered an old-timer, but he continued to play even though the *New York Clipper* commented on his looking "rather rusty" in the field.

Without salary or compensation, Manly continued to play with amateur clubs simply for the love of the game. He disappeared from the baseball stage in the 1870s, and sometime after his death in 1901, his Green-Wood monument disappeared as well.

This woodcut adorned the cover of Frank Queen's *New York Clipper* depicting the scene at Long Island's Fashion Race Course matches of 1858. It was the first season after the formation of the National Association of Base Ball Players, and their sanctioning of this first series of championship matches at the 1858 convention promoted the game and resulted in increased attendance. They were baseball's first official all-star games, and their success laid the foundation for future interest in postseason championship series for years to come.

John B. Holder was a noted cricket player and a star of the original Atlantic Club. He later joined the Excelsiors, and his selection for the grand matches of 1858 was a testament to his skill and his status as a fan favorite. One such fan placed a $100 wager before the first match on his belief that Holder would hit a home run. After his wager was made, the fan told Holder of his plan, and in order to motivate him, offered Holder half of his winnings should the player deliver a home run. (Courtesy of the National Baseball Hall of Fame Library, Cooperstown, New York.)

Newspaper reports of that day in 1858 stated, "Holder was the only one who made a clear home strike, and a beauty it was, clear out of the middle field, which brought him to the home base amidst the most unbounded applause." He left the Fashion Race Course that day $50 richer, and luckily for him, the *Spirit of the Times* reported that "pickpockets were scarce."

Philanthropist and inventor Peter Cooper established the Cooper Union in 1859 as a school of engineering and science as well as a venue for public lectures and gatherings. Located near Astor Place in Manhattan, the school hosted the Lincoln-Douglas presidential debates in 1859, and the National Association of Base Ball Players held their first annual meeting in the lecture hall on March 9 of that same year. Upon motions of the clubs, the officers of 1858 were reelected and the constitution and rules and regulations of the game were revised and amended. The body returned to Cooper's building in 1860, with president William Van Cott presiding over a membership that included a who's who of Green-Wood baseball figures, including Dr. J.B. Jones, Thomas Dakin, Theodore Jackson, John W. Mott, Thomas Voorhis, Dr. William H. Bell, Nelson Shaurman, David Milliken, and Gus Dayton.

Charles Dana was the acting vice president of Brooklyn's Olympic Club in the late 1850s. Some 50 years later, he joined his fellow club members Henry Smith, Charles Marvin, and Charles Rushmore at Green-Wood.

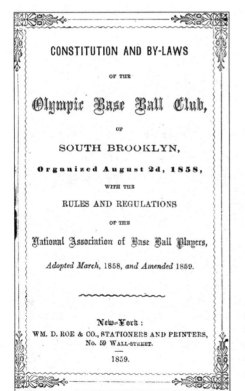

CONSTITUTION AND BY-LAWS

OF THE

Olympic Base Ball Club,

OF

SOUTH BROOKLYN,

Organized August 2d, 1858,

WITH THE

RULES AND REGULATIONS

OF THE

National Association of Base Ball Players,

Adopted March, 1858, and Amended 1859.

New-York:

WM. D. ROE & CO., STATIONERS AND PRINTERS,
No. 59 WALL-STREET.

1859.

Aside from the traditional Brooklyn powerhouses such as the Atlantic, Putnam, and Excelsior Clubs, the association was accepting applications of new clubs at a rapid pace. New teams like the Olympic Club of South Brooklyn were organizing and printing their own bylaws and constitutions, including the one shown here.

David Milliken served as president of the National Association of Base Ball Players in 1861 while a member of the Unions of Morrisania. They first organized in 1855 in what later became a section of the Bronx not far from the future site of old Yankee Stadium. William Cauldwell, owner of the New York *Sunday Mercury* and mentor of Henry Chadwick, served as the club's secretary under Milliken, and both helped the team develop into one of the most successful clubs of the 1860s. Pictured here is Milliken's gated plot at Green-Wood, located directly across from the massive mausoleum of piano manufacturer Steinway.

This oil painting shows the 1866 Unions of Morrisania, the champions of the United States, and features future Hall of Famer George Wright (fourth from the left). The club flourished in the early days under Milliken, who also stood on the National Association's Committee on Nominations that same year. Milliken stands in the center of the painting dressed in street clothes.

With the success of the Fashion Race Course matches in 1858, writer Henry Chadwick talked his editor, Frank Queen of the *New York Clipper*, into commissioning a silver baseball as a prize for a grand match between New York and Brooklyn all-stars, and he enlisted prominent players and officials to select the teams for what was dubbed as the Great Match for the Silver Ball. Anson B. Taylor, a member of the Mutual Club, helped select the players for the New York team, and he was chosen to play left field along with a young future Hall of Famer named Harry Wright. The game was sanctioned by the National Association. Pictured here is the title page from the association's constitution and bylaws that same year.

CONSTITUTION AND BY-LAWS

OF THE

NATIONAL ASSOCIATION

OF

Base Ball Players,

WITH THE

RULES AND REGULATIONS

OF THE

GAME OF BASE BALL.

ADOPTED MARCH, 1858. AMENDED MARCH, 1859 AND '60, AND DECEMBER, 1860.

Published by order of the Association.

New York:

WILBUR & HASTINGS, STATIONERS AND PRINTERS, No. 39 FULTON STREET.

1861.

Brooklyn defeated the New York all-stars 18-6 and left Hoboken's Elysian Fields with the trophy. Anson Taylor, although defeated that day, remained a prominent member of the Mutual Club. By the late 1860s, he was a seasoned veteran who had already seen his best days. As the *New York Clipper* noted, "Ance was at one time considered [by] 'some' as first in the field, but now contents himself as a looker on in Venice." Taylor's family monument at Green-Wood is pictured here.

Brothers Sam and Joe Patchen began their careers as founding members of the Alert Club in 1856. In 1858, they joined their younger brother Edward as members of the Star of Brooklyn Club. Henry Chadwick considered Sam the game's best shortstop next to Dickie Pearce of the Atlantics. Joe was a credible right fielder, and Edward was known to play skillfully at different positions in the infield. This 1859 box score featuring the Patchens illustrates how Henry Chadwick first incorporated base hits, assists, and errors into his match reports.

In 1860, both Sam and Joe Patchen jumped to the Charter Oak Club of Brooklyn, while Edward stayed with the Stars. Sam Patchen was also a member of the Brooklyn City Guard and served in the Civil War for the famed 13th Regiment. Years later, the Patchen brothers were reunited in this impressive vault, built into the slopes of Green-Wood Cemetery's Tulip Hill, just a few hundred feet from the monument of their old teammate Jim Creighton. The epitaphs on the vault can be seen through the ornate iron door.

Five

THE EXCELSIORS AND
THE GREAT REBELLION

Brooklyn's first baseball club and premier nine of the early 1860s was the Excelsior Club of South Brooklyn. John H. Suydan organized the club as the Jolly Young Bachelors Club on the evening of December 8, 1854. They played their first match against the Putnams in 1855, but, as *Porter's Spirit of the Times* reported, they were "not fairly formed until May of 1856." The team flourished through the late 1850s as they joined forces with the Wayne Club and established their home field southeast of Carroll Park. However, it was not until 1860, when pitcher Jim Creighton Jr. joined the club, that the Excelsiors began to dominate the sport. The club embarked on baseball's first tour of match play, traveling the Eastern seaboard to challenge clubs from Philadelphia to Buffalo and defeating all comers. Henry Chadwick considered their tour baseball's "voyage of life" as they introduced the game to new territories. He credited them with doing "more to establish base ball on a permanent and reputable footing than had before been attempted by any other club." (Courtesy of the National Baseball Hall of Fame Library, Cooperstown, New York.)

James Creighton Jr. began his career in 1856 with the Star of Brooklyn Club and joined the Excelsiors in 1860. He was baseball's dominant pitcher, but he was also known for his versatility in the field and at bat. Henry Chadwick wrote, "Not one player in five thousand has the capacity to fill all positions ably and excel in each, the ability required being too great except for one like the admirable Creighton." A baseball phenomenon, Creighton was the first player to achieve celebrity status. His tragic death also gave rise to one of baseball's first myths, that Creighton dramatically died after hitting a home run. In reality, he most likely sustained an injury in a cricket match versus the Willow Club on October 9, 1862, and further aggravated his condition against the Union Club on October 14. He hit two doubles against the Unions, but no home runs. His death was most likely the result of a strangulated intestine. The Excelsiors solidified his place in baseball history with the game's first monument, pictured here.

Across the face of the Creighton monument's column is an intricate design surrounded by oak leaves that were cut into the granite. The design includes a pair of crossed baseball bats, a baseball cap, a base, and a score book featured prominently in the center. The circular emblem is accentuated by a flourishing scroll with the word "Excelsior" carved into it.

After Creighton collapsed during the Union match, his Excelsior teammates carried him back to his father's residence at 307 Henry Street in Brooklyn Heights (pictured as it looks today). He died there just four days later, on October 18, 1862. All of Brooklyn mourned his death.

James Creighton was not the game's only unfortunate casualty in the early 1860s, as the baseball fraternity also lost another player in his prime, George Havemeyer of the Putnam Club. An heir to the Havemeyer sugar fortune, he was accidentally killed in his family's Williamsburg sugar factory. He is buried in his family's underground vault that stretches beneath Green-Wood's Orchard Hill.

John Wesley Cornwell played for the Enterprise Club of Brooklyn in the early 1860s and became a member of the Excelsiors as both clubs consolidated in 1867. The *Ball Player's Chronicle* noted Cornwell's "great physical strength" and how he "ranked high as a player." He drowned tragically on July 4, 1867, at the age of 23, and his *Chronicle* obituary stated, "No event since the death of the much lamented Creighton has created such sorrow." Players from every club marched past his rosewood coffin at the funeral service on Gates Avenue. Having fought in the Union army during the Civil War, he was also honored with the presence of members of Brooklyn's Company B of the 13th Regiment.

In the 140 years that have passed since Creighton's funeral, the unforgiving elements of nature have robbed his monument of its original splendor. The ball that once topped the monument has totally disintegrated, and the detail of the baseball-themed sculpture has eroded. Fortunately for Creighton, Green-Wood Cemetery president Richard J. Moylan has established the Saved in Time historic fund, which will soon restore the monument and summon the return of its long-lost ball.

A BALL PLAYER'S MONUMENT

It Marks the Resting Place in Green-wood of James Creighton.

CREIGHTON

CREIGHTON'S MONUMENT AT GREENWOOD.

did, along with George H. Flanly, who had also been playing with the Niagaras.

When this drawing appeared in the *Brooklyn Daily Eagle* at the turn of the 20th century, Creighton's monument was still topped by "a baseball fashioned in stone" that was first placed there in 1862. The newspaper reported: "On the crest of Tulip Hill, in one of the most picturesque portions of Green-Wood, a striking granite monument marks the spot where one of Brooklyn's pioneer ballplayers lies buried. It is over the grave of Jim Creighton . . . and it would never be mistaken for anything else than a grave of a ball player."

John B. Woodward was a talented player for the Excelsiors, but his duties in the 13th Regiment kept him from devoting more time to baseball. Woodward reached the rank of second lieutenant, and soon after, President Lincoln called his regiment to the front to defend the Union. The 13th Regiment featured a host of his Excelsior mates, the most prominent being star player Joe Leggett. Henry Chadwick once said that the Excelsiors sent close to 90 players into battle during the Civil War.

Leggett and Woodward (seated from left to right) traded in their Excelsior uniforms for Union blues as the war raged. Leggett served as a major under Woodward, who referred to him as "the very best fellow in the entire universe." Woodward commanded troops in the first firing in Virginia, including Sgt. Samuel Kissam of the Knickerbockers, Sam Patchen of the Star, Nelson Shaurman of the Charter Oak, and Morgan Bulkeley, the future National League president and Hall of Famer. Woodward ultimately achieved the rank of general and later was named president of his beloved Excelsior Club.

Young soldiers in the Union army, like 17-year-old Brooklyn resident Charles T. Norris, (his Green-Wood headstone is pictured here) passed what little spare time they had playing baseball. Often, soldiers sent letters back home chronicling their matches against other regiments, like the one below, published in the *Brooklyn Daily Eagle* from the scorer of Brooklyn's "bully 14th boys," who featured Norris in center field.

Base Ball.

BASE BALL IN THE ARMY.—A correspondent favors us with the following letter, containing an account of a match played between a nine from the 14th Regiment of this city, and the 24th Regiment, from which it will be seen that the "bully 14th's boys" not only enjoyed a game of ball but also gained a victory by a good score of 25 to 4. The account is as follows:

To the Editor of the Brooklyn Daily Eagle:

SIR—Enclosed you will find score of a match of base ball played Monday, Nov. 25th, on our parade ground, between the 14th Regiment of Brooklyn and the 24th Regiment N. Y. V., which resulted in a complete victory for the Brooklyn boys, after playing five innings, which closed the game on account of its being parade time. We will play the return match next week if we don't move from where we are at present. Very respectfully,

SCORER 14TH REGT. B. B. C.

The score was as appended.

14TH REGT. B. B. C.	H.L.	R.	24TH REGT. B. B. G.	H.L.	R.
J. A. Brown, c,	2	3	W. Shephard, p	0	1
W. Van Pelt,	3	2	M. Crowell, c f	3	0
A. Travis, 1st b,	2	3	A. Phillips, 1st b	1	2
W. Brockett, 2d b	2	2	Walter Brownell, c	3	0
J. H. Young, 3d b	2	2	W. R. Browne, r f	0	0
A. Snediker, s s	1	3	R. R. Browne, 3d b	3	0
J. R. Bennett, l f	1	3	P. O. Wright, 2d b	3	0
C. T. Norrie, c f,	2	2	G. Kingsley l f	2	0
J. Long, r f	0	4	J. Walrath, s s	0	1
Totals	15	25	Totals	15	4

RUNS MADE IN EACH INNING.

	1st	2d	3d	4th	5th	6th	7th	8th	9th	
14th Regt.	2	0	3	12	2					—25
24th Regt.	2	0	1	1	0					— 4

Umpire—W. H. Adriance, Esq., of the Frontier Club, of Oswego.

Scorer for the 24th Regiment—Mr. S. H. Hastings.

Scorer for the 14th Regiment—Mr. S. H. Stratford.

Home runs—Brown, 1; Van Pelt, 1; Brocket, 1; Bennet, 1.

On their parade grounds at an undisclosed location, the 14th Regiment players battered the 24th Regiment from upstate New York 24-5 in just five innings, until their match was interrupted by "parade time." Green-Wood is home to thousands of Civil War veterans. Joining center fielder Norris are teammates James Long, John Bennett, and John A. Brown.

Abram Duryee, a Civil War general now buried at Green-Wood, commanded a regiment of close to 1,000 men of the Fifth New York Volunteers, known as the "Duryee Zouves." His men fought hard in many campaigns, including Second Bull Run, where Duryee was wounded twice. As the war progressed, the 165th and 4th Regiments were thereafter called "the second Duryee Zouaves." On the right is the Civil War soldiers' monument on Green-Wood's Battle Hill. (Courtesy of Jeffrey Richman.)

One soldier in the 165th Regiment was future National League president A.G. Mills, who recalled playing in a match on Christmas Day 1862 against a team of other Union regiments. Although Mills was probably exaggerating, he claimed the game was witnessed by more than 40,000 soldiers who had gathered in Hilton Head, South Carolina. Matches like this one illustrate how the war helped spread the game far and wide. The Christmas-day match featuring the 165th would have resembled the image above, which depicts Union prisoners playing baseball in Salisbury, North Carolina. (Courtesy of the National Baseball Hall of Fame Library, Cooperstown, New York.)

In December 1860, Nelson Shaurman represented Brooklyn's Charter Oak Club as their delegate to the National Association's convention at New York's Cooper Union. He was a police captain by profession, and by April 1861, his baseball career was interrupted when he was called to serve in the Brooklyn City Guard. He was elevated to colonel of Brooklyn's 19th Regiment and was eventually appointed general by brevet for his service in New York's 90th Infantry.

DELEGATES TO ASSOCIATION.

Knickerbocker...	{	D. L. ADAMS, WM. H. GRENELLE.
Gotham......	{	WM. H. VAN COTT, S. VAN WINKLE,
Eagle....	{	A. J. BIXBY, CHAS. PLACE, JR.
Empire............	{	T. G. VOORHIS, JAMES CAMERON.
Putnam.....	{	THOS. S. DAKIN, THEO. F. JACKSON.
Baltic....	{	P. WEEKS, W. S. PINCKNEY.
Excelsior.....	{	J. B. JONES, J. B. LEGGETT.
Atlantic.....	{	G. F. BARNARD, F. K. BOUGHTON.
Harlem....	{	C. W. VAN VOORHIS, THOS. BELL.
Eckford......	{	FRANCIS PIDGEON, E. JENKINS.

Nelson Shaurman stood beside baseball's founding fathers at the early National Association of Base Ball Players meetings. Pictured here is a page from the 1861 association constitution and bylaws listing him "on nomination" amongst fellow Green-Wood pioneers William Van Cott, Thomas Voorhis, Thomas Dakin, Theodore Jackson, Dr. Joseph B. Jones, and F.K. Boughton.

Dr. Joseph B. Jones joined the Excelsior Club in 1858 with fellow surgeon Aleck Pearsall after both had left Brooklyn's Aesculapian Club. He became club orator and president and was instrumental in the formulation of the association rules along with Doc Adams of the Knickerbockers. Henry Chadwick also worked closely with Jones on the association's Standing Committee on Rules. In 1860, Jones was elected president of the National Association of Base Ball Players, and when the Civil War commanded the nation's full attention, baseball continued in Brooklyn under his leadership. Dr. Jones proposed a special resolution to the association that any surplus funds in their accounts should be distributed pro rata to every ballplayer serving in Union regiments. Dr. Jones, upon his death in 1905, found himself in the shadow of the Green-Wood monument of Horace Greeley, famed *New York Tribune* founder and editor (pictured above in the distance).

Dr. Jones (in a top hat) poses here in 1859 with outfielder Harry Polhemus, regarded in the *New York Clipper* as "an excellent fielder in the good old times, [who could] yet handle the ash in 'Excelsior' style." Polhemus hailed from one of Brooklyn's founding families and his ancestors included Rev. Johannes Theodorus Polhemus, Brooklyn's first ordained minister, and Theodorus Polhemus, Bushwick's representative to "the Provincial Congress at New York in 1775 and 1776." (Courtesy of the National Baseball Hall of Fame Library, Cooperstown, New York.)

Henry D. Polhemus was a mainstay of the early Excelsior team. He was a millionaire in his day and a close friend of Pres. Grover Cleveland. When he was not playing ball, he served on the board of regents at Long Island College Hospital. Henry Chadwick regularly commented on his generosity and donations to charity. He stood on the Excelsior committee to honor Creighton in 1862, and in 1895, he too was interred in one of the oldest family plots at Green-Wood. In his memory, his widow bequeathed $500,000 to Long Island College Hospital to establish the Polhemus Dispensary building, which still stands.

Frank Cowperthwait served as the Excelsior team captain and treasurer, while his brother assumed the duties as club vice president. Frank usually served as the club's catcher, and Bernard covered positions in the Excelsior infield. The brothers' tenure as Excelsiors marked the developmental stages of the organization more as a junior club—a far cry from the dominant nine of the years to come.

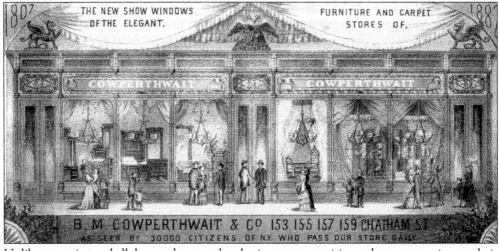

Unlike most pioneer ballplayers who passed up business opportunities to devote more time to their clubs, Bernard Cowperthwait emerged as a prominent and wealthy furniture manufacturer and merchant with large showrooms in both Brooklyn and New York City. This trade card from the 1880s is a testament to his success, as it proclaimed "30,000 New Yorkers pass our store daily."

Henry W. Maxwell grew up following the exploits of the Excelsior baseball clubs of the early 1860s. By the decade's end, he was a full-fledged club member and competed on the field with the likes of Harry Polhemus, William Kendall, and Gen. John B. Woodward.

Maxwell was named president of the Excelsior Club and later became a staunch supporter of professional ball in Brooklyn. He was famous for funding various charities and financial projects in the city. After attending Maxwell's 1902 funeral at Green-Wood, Henry Chadwick published a poem about his old friend:

His years but young, but his experience old:
His head unmellowed, but his
Judgment ripe. And in a word-
For far behind his worth come all
The praises that I now bestow-
He was complete in feature and in mind
With all good grace to grace a gentleman.

75

William B. Kendall, like Henry Maxwell, was a popular Excelsior who played faithfully on the club's second string. By the late 1850s, he was an integral part of their operation and worked under the president, Dr. J.B. Jones, as the club secretary.

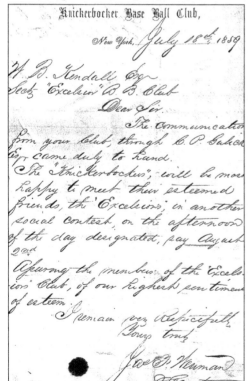

This letter was sent to Excelsior Club secretary William Kendall by fellow Green-Wood legend James Wenman of the Knickerbocker Club to accept an invitation to engage in a match. The Knick and Excelsior matches of 1858 and 1859 were historic in that the teams played under the fly rule instead of the bound, which was then in vogue. (Courtesy of the Spalding Baseball Collection, New York Public Library.)

The Excelsior clubhouse still stands at the corner of Clinton and Livingston Streets in Brooklyn Heights. The structure, now a co-op, serves as home to a number of different families. It once served as the focal point for all club activities in Jim Creighton's heyday, but by 1874, it was officially incorporated as a social club. In 1878, the club dropped the words "base ball" altogether from its name.

The New York City landmark plaque affixed to the front of the old clubhouse building reads, in part: "Constructed in 1851 the building was once the 'Jolly Young Bachelor's Clubhouse.' The Bachelors evolved into the Excelsior baseball team."

Brooklyn's Chauncey brothers, George and Daniel, were two of the Excelsiors' best players, and like Harry Polhemus, they were considered the wealthiest in the baseball ranks. George became president of the Excelsior social club but never quite got the baseball bug out of his system. In 1890, as players from the National League revolted against their owners, George bankrolled the Brooklyn Player's League team and enlisted the services of John Ward as a player-manager. The league quickly went bust, but George got a second chance in the game when he purchased an ownership interest in the Brooklyn Club. It was Chauncey who first offered Charles Ebbets, the team secretary, a piece of the team in the form of club stock. According to Frank Graham's *The Brooklyn Dodgers*, he told the young Ebbets, "I am selling it to you because I know that owning it will be an even greater spur to you—that it will make you work even harder than you have so far, if that's possible." George Chauncey was a very substantial man, and along with his Excelsior brother Daniel, he was honored at Green-Wood with a very substantial monument.

Six

THE MIGHTY ATLANTICS

Dear Eagle:
I am beginning to take an interest in our national game. Which is baseball. Our noble city, third in population and first in Base Ball, has been glorified in field sports by the Atlantic Club, who have whipped everything in the ball line. As a Brooklynite, I am proud of the Atlantics. There are nine of them. They are wonderfully smart fellows. Stand six feet two in their stockings, can run two miles a minute, jump over a forty foot fence, or through a knot hole, turn a somersault and catch anything from a base ball to the measles. They are an honor to Brooklyn.

This passage appeared in "Corry O'Lanus' Epistle," in the *Brooklyn Daily Eagle* of September 4, 1865. By that time, the nation was emerging from the Civil War and the Atlantic Club had assumed the position of the top nine in the "City of Churches" and beyond. The contingent featured above included a formidable lineup of future Green-Wood occupants such as Fred Crane (left), Jack Chapman (second from the left), and Charles Smith (third from the left). Club manager Peter O'Brien is seated in the center, and Sid Smith is second from the right.

Jack Chapman began his career on Brooklyn's Putnam Club and moved to the Enterprise in 1861. He was the first to attempt daring, one-hand, running fly catches. At bat, he was considered one of baseball's first true power hitters. The *New York Clipper* described his versatility as "a quick batsman, a long distance thrower, a sure catch and an effective slow pitcher." When he died in 1916, his loss was mourned throughout Brooklyn and his brother Elks from Lodge No. 22 handled his funeral arrangements.

Having attended Henry Chadwick's 1909 monument dedication, Chapman might have borrowed the father of baseball's motif for the large sculpted ball that topped the monument of his own family plot. Pictured here is the copy of the cemetery work order to replace his family monument with the one pictured above. The order was placed in May 1909, just weeks after Chapman attended the unveiling of the Chadwick monument.

Brooklyn, N. Y. _May_ 190 9.

Superintendent

The Green-Wood Cemetery.

Please allow _John Feitner_
to _Erect Monument and_
remove small stone
in Lot _28654_ Sec. _165_

John C. Chapman

In 1875, Chapman was selected as the St. Louis Club's player-manager. By 1877, he retired and assumed managerial duties for Louisville. Four of his players that season sold out to gamblers by throwing numerous games and ultimately the pennant. It was the National League's first scandal. Chapman recovered and went on to manage, coach, and scout for decades. His managerial record was a mediocre 351-502, but he did win a pennant with Louisville in 1890. He also had a great eye for talent and discovered Hall of Famers Hughie Jennings and Jimmy Collins.

Chapman took part in the famous 1870 match between the Atlantics and the undefeated Cincinnati Red Stockings, manning right field as they battled the Reds to a tie score after nine innings. The crowd of more than 10,000 knew that a tie would end the Cincinnati streak. Chapman scurried onto the field to collect the team bats while Red Stocking Harry Wright argued with Henry Chadwick for extra innings. Wright won the argument, but the Atlantics prevailed in 11 innings by a score of 8-7. Not only did Chapman and his teammates end the Red Stockings' record streak of victories, they also pocketed $364 each from the Capitoline Grounds gate receipts.

Fred Crane began his career with the Enterprise Club, and he replaced Johnny Oliver at second base for the Atlantics in 1863. Crane was highly regarded as a great fielder, hitter, and base runner. The *New York Clipper* called him "the most graceful as well as a sure and active fielder." His fielding was legendary, and reports of the day claimed, "When a ball is knocked in his neighborhood, off goes Fred's cap, and he takes the ball in so easy a manner that fails not to draw applause." He was noted for his ability to turn quick double plays with shortstop Dickie Pearce.

A man of many talents, Fred Crane's skills were not just confined to the ball field. He was also an accomplished singer in a Brooklyn choir. On the road, he and Jack Chapman made quite a team as Crane sang to Jack's accomplished whistling, for which he had gained quite a national reputation while traveling with the club. Crane later went into business in New York City manufacturing machinery but continued to live in Brooklyn as Henry Chadwick's neighbor on Halsey Street. Both Crane and Chapman are now buried in Green-Wood Cemetery.

Sidney C. Smith played his junior ball with the Star of Brooklyn Club in the early 1860s and first became connected with the champion Atlantics in 1864. He remained with the club until 1866. As their trusty right fielder, Smith was an integral part of their successful run as champions of America.

When Sid Smith retired from the diamond, he moved on to earn an honest living at the Kings County tax office. Smith died at the age of 65. His family monument is pictured here.

As was the custom in 19th-century baseball, the game ball was awarded to the winning team as a trophy of their victory. The Atlantics amassed hundreds of them, and their club manager, Mike Henry, constructed an elaborate display case to house the balls, which were painted white with blue lettering that recorded the details of each contest. It was the centerpiece of their clubhouse at Henry's place on Fulton Street and later moved to the Willoughby Shades Bar on Adams Street. The case was maintained for years by Paul Mead and Atlantic player Humphrey Hartshorn until it returned to Henry's new tavern on Boerum Place. Sadly, Henry died in 1889 as a pauper in the Flatbush Insane Asylum, and the case, always on loan from the club itself, moved to the Niagara House on Court Street, which was owned by John Campbell. After Campbell closed out the business, he gave the case to sporting promoter Charley Johnston without consulting the surviving club members. Atlantic members such as Jack Chapman were infuriated and pleaded with Johnston to return the case to the club. Johnston seemed agreeable to the plan, but he died in 1905 before any transfer, thus leaving the ownership claim to the case in question. (Courtesy of the Spalding Baseball Collection, New York Public Library.)

Charley Johnston gained renown as the backer of boxer John L. Sullivan, but he was a reported lover of baseball as well. The *Brooklyn Daily Eagle* called him "the backbone of the old Atlantic Base Ball Club," although he never played the game. By the time he was buried in Green-Wood, his demise had set off a firestorm as club members pleaded with his family to donate the case to the Brooklyn Institute (now the Brooklyn Museum). Years later, the case came into the possession of the Brooklyn Club and ended up for years on display with other baseball relics in the rotunda of Dodger owner Charles Ebbets's new stadium, Ebbets Field.

True-blue Dodger fans cringe at the mention of Walter O'Malley, who moved their beloved team from the borough. O'Malley not only broke the hearts of Dodger fans, he literally broke open the Atlantic trophy case as well, giving balls out to departing employees as tokens of appreciation. Today, the balls have resurfaced in the most unlikely of places. In this photograph, an auctioneer sells off the last vestiges of Ebbets Field and, quite possibly, the remaining Atlantic trophy balls.

Charles J. Smith (sixth from the left) made his debut with the Atlantics on October 18, 1858, in a match with the Putnam Club. He remained their third baseman for a decade. His powerful throwing arm, his agility in getting under fly balls, and his general quickness made him one of the most formidable players of his era. He was a powerful batsman and the mainstay of the championship teams of the 1860s. Fellow player C. Stanton Smith once called him "the greatest player of his time." Charles Smith left baseball after the 1870 campaign, but he decided to return in 1871 as a professional member of the New York Mutuals. He opened the season but was sidelined due to a mental disorder. Although he fully recovered, the episode forced the veteran to retire for good. Smith moved to a farm in Great Neck on Long Island and spent the remainder of his life in relative obscurity as a breeder of dogs. When he died in the fall of 1897, he was buried in what appeared to be an unmarked grave at Green-Wood Cemetery. (Courtesy of the National Baseball Hall of Fame Library, Cooperstown, New York.)

Baseball legend Charlie Smith appeared to have been buried, like so many other ballplayers, in an unmarked grave. However, research of cemetery records yielded proof of a headstone being located at his grave between 1897 and 1919. With the assistance of Green-Wood's Richard Sneddon and a crew of cemetery gravediggers (pictured here), Smith's monument was discovered a few feet underground. Without a proper foundation, the headstone had sunk over the years. Thanks to the assistance of Sneddon and the cemetery crew, the monument, marked only by the name "Charlie," has been restored to its original state for the first time in over a century.

Base Ball.

Return match of the Atlantic and Harmony clubs, played on the ground of the latter.

ATLANTIC.		HARMONY.	
T. Powers	3	Bergen	2
Whitson	4	Phelps	1
C. Sniffen	2	Boerum	1
T. Hamilton	3	Ireland	2
J. Loper	4	Price	1
W. Babcock	4	Robbins	1
W. Bliss	2	McCoy	1
J. Holder	3	Backman	0
A. Gildersleive	2	Roper	1
Total	27	Total	10

This box score dating from 1855 is for the second match ever played by the Atlantics. Their opponent was the newly formed Harmony Club, which featured prominent cricketer and skillful pitcher George Phelps. The Atlantics were too strong, however, and after a few matches, both clubs decided to consolidate. Folkert Boerum, Len Bergen, and Edward Price became standout members of the club in the years to come.

This image of an early Atlantic team dates from *c.* 1860. The individuals in this carte-de-visite image are, from left to right, the following: (seated) unidentified, Marion Thwaites, and four unidentified men; (standing) Dickie Pearce, unidentified, Charles Smith, unidentified, and Peter O'Brien. The two individuals in formal dress are most likely William Babcock, F.K. Boughton, George Rogers, or club manager Mike Henry. Matty O'Brien, Folkert Boerum, and Johnny Oliver most likely appear in the photograph as well.

Folkert Rapelye Boerum was the Harmony Club's first baseman in 1855 and, in 1856, joined the Atlantics as catcher to their ace, William V. Babcock. Boerum continued with the club as a catcher and third baseman until 1861 and was considered a strong player, having been selected as an all-star in the Fashion Race Course matches of 1858. His ancestor, Simon Boerum, represented Kings County as a member of the first Continental Congress in 1774. Long after his playing days, Boerum attempted unsuccessfully to purchase the Atlantic trophy case from Charley Johnston, hoping to donate it to the Brooklyn Institute.

John Ireland joined the pioneer Harmony Club in 1855 as a teenager and played in both of their inaugural matches with the Atlantics. He never continued with the Atlantics after they merged with the Harmony in 1856, but he went on to achieve considerable success as a Brooklyn businessman and socialite.

Len Bergen was another original member of the Harmony Club but soon joined his other skilled teammates as they merged with the Atlantics in 1856. Green-Wood is filled with many Bergens; the clan had a long history in Brooklyn and even had streets named for them.

Johnnie Oliver was the Atlantic second baseman of the late 1850s and early 1860s. He was considered one of the game's premier players along with his brother Joe, the Atlantic left fielder. John played for Brooklyn in two of the Fashion Race Course matches of 1858 and helped lead them to their only victory in the second match, scoring three runs. He died of consumption quite young in 1869 and was later reunited with Joe in their family plot at Green-Wood.

William M. "Boss" Tweed, the infamous Tammany Hall politician, was the foreman of the famous Americus Engine Company No. 6 (their plot at Green-Wood is pictured above) and later was connected with the Mutual Hook and Ladder Company No. 1. That fire company formed a ball club known as the Mutuals, and Tweed financially backed them throughout the 1860s, at a time when gamblers and criminality threatened the very fabric of the national game. Firemen such as John Wildey were Tweed confidants. Wildey went on to star for the Mutual Club as one of their finest players and starred in many of their great matches against the rival Atlantics.

John Wildey was a distinguished firefighter who was often referred to in the baseball press as "Coroner Wildey" for the position he held as city coroner in Boss Tweed's administration. He also served as the Mutual Club's president, managing a roster of city workers who sometimes were paid with public funds for their ball playing. Coroner Wildey joined Tweed at Green-Wood in 1889. He lies in an unmarked grave.

Asa Brainard began his career with his brother Harrison as a member of the Brooklyn Excelsiors, playing alongside the legendary James Creighton in the early 1860s. He remained with the Excelsiors until 1866 and made the pilgrimage to Creighton's monument with the visiting Washington Nationals that same year. By 1867, he was recruited by and joined the Nationals, who unofficially compensated him for his services with a government job. Within a year, he joined the Cincinnati Red Stockings as their club pitcher.

Seven

BASEBALL'S FIRST
PROFESSIONALS

The champion Cincinnati Red Stocking Club of 1869 featured the dazzling pitching skills of Brooklyn's own Asa Brainard (seated second from the right). He was accustomed to being paid for his services, although that was not the common practice of the amateur game. In 1868, when Brainard was 28 years of age, Cincinnati manager Harry Wright recruited him to join the Red Stockings, offering him an annual salary of $1,100. Wright's offer to Brainard and other players, including Wright's brother George, constituted the framework for the first openly professional club. With Brainard at the helm, the team began to dominate, and in 1869, they toured the country and challenged every significant club they could find. They remained undefeated until the season's end and created a groundswell of interest in the game never before seen. Brainard was known as the Red Stockings' "ace" pitcher, and the phrase has survived to this day, used when describing a team's best pitcher.

Brainard contracted smallpox shortly after he arrived in Cincinnati. He was boarding at the home of Mary Truman, a wealthy widow whose late husband was a partner in the printing company that established McGuffey Readers. She tended to Brainard day and night until he finally recovered from the illness. The sickly Brainard and his nurse soon became romantically involved and were married shortly before the baseball season commenced.

Brainard's marriage was an unhappy one, and after deserting his wife and child in the 1870s, he resurfaced in 1882 as the operator of an archery range on Staten Island. Reports indicate that Asa suffered a painful archery injury when he was struck on his hand with an arrow. Brainard was always fond of pool halls, and he moved out west and again resurfaced as a manager of a billiard hall in Denver, Colorado, where he met an early death in 1888.

Brainard left the Reds after the 1870 season, as they soon disbanded when public support and investors dried up after their winning streak ended in Brooklyn at the hand of the Atlantics. With the formation of the new National Association of Base Ball Players, Brainard relocated to Washington, D.C., and joined the Olympic Club. Uncharacteristically, he struggled in the box, as his pitching skill was a mere shadow of what it was for the champion Reds.

A.W. Gedney was nicknamed "the Count." He was one of many trailblazers who helped establish the National Association of Professional Base Ball Players. Gedney began his playing career in the late 1860s with the Unions of Morrisania and later played for the Brooklyn Eckfords and Troy Haymakers in 1872, the New York Mutuals in 1873, the Philadelphia Athletics in 1874, and, finally, went back to the Mutuals in 1875.

In July 1874, Gedney accompanied his Philadelphia teammates on an international baseball tour to England at the behest of Albert Spalding and Harry Wright of the Boston Club. Gedney appeared in 54 games for the Athletics, playing in the outfield alongside future Hall of Famer Cap Anson. He scored 48 runs and hit safely 76 times as he accumulated a batting average of .323 for the season. (Courtesy of the National Baseball Hall of Fame Library, Cooperstown, New York.)

George Fletcher was another one of the game's first professionals who got an initial taste of playing for pay with the Nationals of Washington, D.C. He worked as a clerk in D.C.'s third auditor's office while playing catcher for the touring baseball club along with Hall of Famer George Wright. In 1867, he led the club in put outs and was second only to Wright in total bases on hits. By the time the National Association of Base Ball Players formed, he was back in Brooklyn playing for the Eckfords.

Some of baseball's first professionals lie in relative obscurity in various unmarked graves and family plots that make no visible reference to the names of the deceased players, let alone mark their baseball careers. Dick Hunt was the 145-pound right fielder for the professional Brooklyn Eckfords. He hit .288 for the club in 1872, and by 1895, he was at Green-Wood in his father's plot, pictured here.

BASE-BALL PLAYER.

NEW YORK.

BEADLE AND COMPANY, 118 WILLIAM ST.
The American News Co., 121 Nassau St., N. Y.

In 1859, Robert Adams and Irwin Beadle founded the operation that revolutionized the American literary scene with their wildly popular dime novels. In 1860, operating as the firm of Irwin Beadle and Company, the duo commissioned Henry Chadwick to write manuals on both baseball and cricket. With their publication of his work, the game spread like wildfire throughout the country. Chadwick presented the rules and regulations of the game and also included detailed instructions on how players could form their own club.

Henry Chadwick's relationship with Beadle and Adams prospered for many years; however, Robert Adams's fate was much more precarious. He died tragically in 1866 at the age of 29.

Eight

THE BUSINESS OF BASEBALL

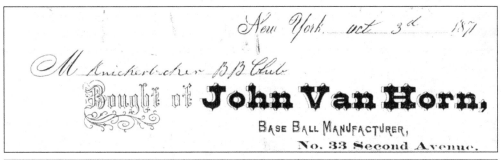

John Van Horn played second base for New York's Baltic Club in the 1850s and was a shoemaker by trade. Having developed considerable sewing talents in shoemaking, he easily incorporated his skills to become the most prolific ball maker of the 19th century. The Knickerbockers and other topnotch clubs purchased balls and bats at his shop on Second Avenue. His advertisement in the *New York Clipper* described the distinctive trademark he used on his creations: "John Van Horn, No. 33 Second Avenue, New York." The greatest ball maker of them all, Van Horn lies in an unmarked grave in a public section of the cemetery. The illustration depicts a ball maker in the 1860s. (Top image courtesy of the Spalding Baseball Collection, New York Public Library.)

Harvey Ross was a sailmaker by trade and an active member of the Atlantic Club in Brooklyn. He made baseballs for the club beginning in the 1860s. At a time when teams furnished their own balls for matches, word spread about Ross's ball-making skill, and in no time, he had established his own business at 224 Park Avenue in Brooklyn. The above advertisement from the late 1860s describes the distinctive stamp Ross emblazoned on each of his products and warned buyers of the proliferation of counterfeits. The Atlantics favored the Ross ball. Soon, clubs all over the country were using his horsehide spheres.

This lonely public lot on the outskirts of Green-Wood holds the remains of legendary ball maker Harvey Ross.

James F. Marsters operated one of the largest sporting-goods houses in the nation and boasted of having the most attractive catalog of sporting goods in the country. His specialty was the manufacture of baseball uniforms, including caps, shirts, belts, pants, stockings, shoes, and spikes. He also kept in stock baseballs from most manufacturers. By the late 1870s, Marsters could not compete with the likes of A.G. Spalding Brothers and Company, who had secured official contracts with the National League and began to buy out his competition.

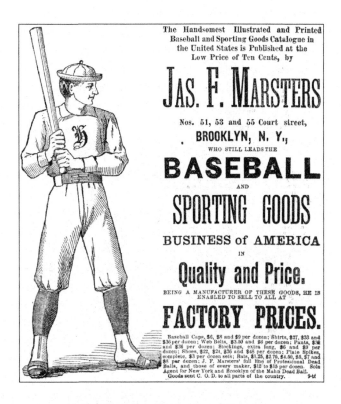

After the baseball magnates took over the baseball sporting-goods business, Marsters retreated to a small operation that specialized in fishing tackle. He died in 1906 and was buried in Green-Wood beneath the monument pictured here.

Edward I. Horsman was a well-respected Brooklynite and a renowned importer, dealer, and manufacturer of toys and games in New York City. By the 1890s, he was considered the country's leader in wholesale toy trading. He got his start constructing lemon-peeled horsehide baseballs by hand.

At age 19, E.I. Horsman began noticing the growing fervor over baseball in Brooklyn and, soon after, experimented with ways to become more formally associated with the sport. He began to make his own baseballs, working with yarn, rubber cuttings, and thread to handcraft each one to perfection. By 1870, Horsman boasted that he had the oldest baseball retail store in the country.

THE OLDEST ESTABLISHED

BASE-BALL EMPORIUM

IN THE UNITED STATES.

E. I. HORSMAN,

100 William Street, New York,

MANUFACTURER AND DEALER IN

BASE-BALLS, BATS, BASES,

SCORE-BOOKS,

CAPS, BELTS, PANTS, SHIRTS,

and everything connected with the game.

CRICKET and ARCHERY Goods of all kinds.

CROQUET in endless variety.

Send STAMP for Circular and Price List.

In 1862, Horsman got his first big break when a silver ball match was scheduled between the Eckford and Atlantic Clubs. Having offered one of his balls for use in the match, both clubs agreed, and the Eckfords gave his creation a beating, scoring eight runs to the Atlantic's three. The *Brooklyn Daily Times* reported that, "The ball used on this occasion was made by E. I. Horsman, well known as a base ball manufacturer, and presented by him for this occasion. These balls are for sale at the base ball depot, 124 South Sixth Street."

Horsman was born in New York City in 1843. When he was three years old, his family moved to Brooklyn, and he remained a resident for the remainder of his life. His sporting-goods empire competed with the likes of Peck and Snyder, Wright and Ditson, Reach and Johnston, and a host of others. However, his involvement in the sale of wholesale toys made him one of the wealthiest members of the New York Chamber of Commerce. His family monument at Green-Wood, pictured here, is representative of the wealth and stature of 19th-century manufacturers with its own granite stairway and figural posts that once held an impressive cast-iron fence that enclosed the plot. During World War II, the cemetery disassembled many of these fences to contribute metal to the war effort.

Alexander Waugh's business was the manufacture of toys and fireworks. He first established his business in 1859 at a facility located at 222 and 224 Ninth Avenue in New York City. He was a prolific manufacturer, who, in just one season (from January to April), reportedly manufactured as many as 2,250,000 kite sticks. He was known famously for his novelties, and his originality and ingenuity propelled him to the forefront of the American toy industry.

Although Peck and Snyder most likely constructed the first dead ball—a baseball with less elasticity and therefore less pop off of a bat—an unattributed 1872 news clipping credits Waugh with the invention. This advertisement from the *New York Clipper* in the early 1870s heralds Waugh's "4X Dead Ball," which was adopted as the official ball of the Junior Convention of the National Association of Base Ball Players.

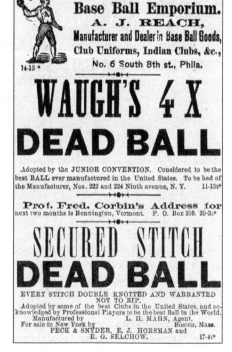

Charles Peverelly became one of the game's earliest historians with the 1866 release of his *Book of American Pastimes*. The *New York Clipper* had commented on the insufficient quantity and quality of sporting literature at the time and eagerly awaited the release of Peverelly's work that November. It was billed as a "complete history of rowing, yachting, base ball and cricket clubs of the United States." His groundbreaking work chronicled baseball's history and was true to many of the views previously taught by Henry Chadwick to younger writers. Years later, writer Will Rankin recalled how Knickerbocker Duncan Curry once stated, "I never saw rounders and never heard of it until Charles Peverelly made the claim in his book." Peverelly's grave is only a few hundred yards from Curry's monument.

Peverelly first wrote on the subject of baseball for the *New York Daily News* in the early 1860s and, along with Henry Chadwick, claimed status as a pioneer baseball scribe. Unfortunately, Peverelly had to abandon his coverage of ball games due to his failing eyesight. His vision, however, could handle a sport like yachting, and he soon recovered from his reportorial hiatus with his establishment of a weekly yachting journal.

Will Rankin entered baseball as a reporter for the *Rockland County Journal* in the early 1870s and simultaneously cut his teeth as a player on amateur nines fielded in Nyack, New York. On the recommendation of Henry Chadwick, he became a city reporter for the New York *Sunday Mercury* and soon augmented his work as the baseball reporter for the *New York Herald*. When Chadwick left the *New York Clipper* in 1888, Rankin assumed the position of assistant editor. By 1894, he was named the *Clipper's* sporting editor.

In 1886, Will Rankin published a syndicated article of his own on the origins of baseball that countered Chadwick's rounders theory. The two butted heads continually from that point on, and in his last years, Chadwick referred to Rankin as his only enemy in the baseball world. Rankin later revealed that, although there was bad blood between them, the grand old man Chadwick visited Rankin in 1908 at his home seeking information for the last guide he edited in his life. Nonetheless, Rankin did whatever he could to discredit Chadwick's deeds and, at times, became consumed by his envy of Chadwick's fame.

Will Rankin died sitting on a crosstown Brooklyn trolley and was buried in this lonely public lot at Green-Wood bordering Brooklyn's 37th Street.

GEORGE E. STACKHOUSE,
The Sporting Life's New York Correspondent.

Born in the wilds of Kentucky, George Stackhouse first came to New York in the winter of 1879 looking for work. The *New York Tribune* employed one of his relatives, and, luckily, he was able to parlay his familial ties into a steady job as a writer. By the spring of 1883, he began covering the baseball beat. Soon after, he earned his nickname "Stack" and branched off to cover other sports and pastimes, including horse racing. As a friend and colleague of Henry Chadwick, he soon established himself as one of the most talented and respected writers on the circuit and was appointed the New York correspondent to Francis Richter's baseball weekly, the *Sporting Life*.

In 1903, George Stackhouse was cut down in his prime. On a writer's meager salary, he never accumulated much wealth. His unmarked grave rests in one of Green-Wood's public burial sections.

Enjoyment and Enlightenment
for
Real Base Ball Fans

The Sporting News

Staff of correspondents includes such noted writers on base ball as

JOE VILA, *Sun*, AND W. M. RANKIN, *Clipper*, NEW YORK.

Joe Vila grew up in New England, entered Harvard in 1889, and was a member of the Crimson football and baseball squads. Although he had secured a varsity position on both teams, Vila quit school and went into business. In 1893, he began his career as a journalist for New York's *Sun* and was the first to report the burial wishes of Knickerbocker James Whyte Davis.

Vila set off a baseball war in 1929. New York City Mayor Jimmy Walker mentioned to publisher Paul Block that he wanted to buy the Brooklyn Club, if only he had the money. Block expressed interest in financing Walker's idea. Vila immediately printed up the story and sent it over to the mayor's office for comment. Walker expressed his hope that the *Sun* would not run the story and threatened that if Vila did, he would deny it and back out of any deal he might have had. Walker made an offer to Brooklyn owner Steve McKeever, but he felt the Brooklyn boys were not giving him the proper respect. Vila respectfully held back the story, but someone leaked it to another paper that went straight to McKeever for his quotation (from Frank Graham's *The Brooklyn Dodgers*), "There isn't enough money in New York City to buy me out of baseball."

Frank Pearsall established himself as one of Brooklyn's premier artistic photographers of the later half of the 19th century. He was also an avid fan of the national game and became close friends with Henry Chadwick. Over the years, Pearsall served as Chadwick's personal photographer and rendered portraits for the "father of the game" each year for his birthday, most of which graced the pages of the annual *Spalding League Guide*.

Frank Pearsall established his first studio in Brooklyn in 1870, and by the early 1880s, Henry Chadwick reported that Pearsall invented a portable camera appropriate for baseball. At that time, Pearsall specialized in portraits of baseball and cricket teams, and he gained the reputation, along with Brooklyn's Joseph Hall, as one of the most prominent baseball portrait photographers.

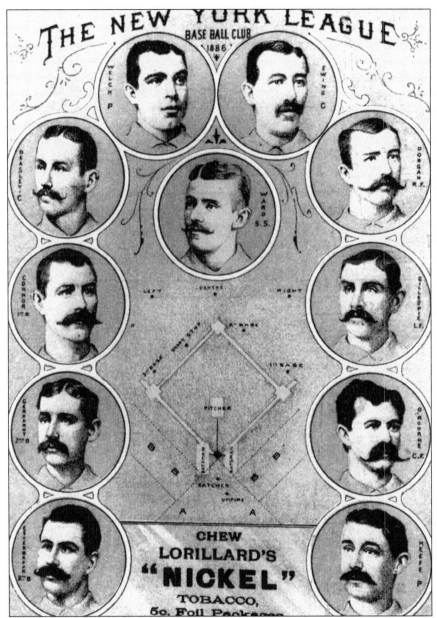

Pierre Lorillard's primary claim to fame was the invention of the tailless jacket that became known around the world as the tuxedo. He made his fortune as a 19th-century tobacco merchant at a time when tobacco was closely associated with the national game. Players and fans alike were avid tobacco fiends, much to the chagrin of sportswriter Henry Chadwick, who actively preached the evils of wine, women, and weed to the ball-playing fraternity. By the 1880s, Lorillard and others capitalized on baseball's popularity by utilizing ballplayers and teams on both their products and promotional materials. In one of the earliest such productions, Lorillard's company offered a set of team cards that featured the portraits of players with their team schedule on the reverse side (pictured above). Of course, it included an advertisement for Lorillard's Climax Plug tobacco. Within a few years, cards similar to Lorillard's established the national popularity of the baseball card, which endures to this day.

Joseph Hall was the most prominent baseball photographer of the Victorian era. National League baseball players visited his Fulton Street studios for posed portraits in uniform, and Hall also travelled with his camera to Brooklyn's Washington Park to photograph visiting clubs. Pictured here is Hall's cabinet-size photograph of Cap Anson's 1888 Chicago Club with thespian and Green-Wood resident DeWolf Hopper (seated third from the right in the front). Hall's team photographs were marketed for public sale in 1888. Today, surviving specimens have sold at public auction for over $10,000.

In the late 1880s, Joseph Hall's photography was purchased by tobacco companies and served as the basis for some of the first baseball cards ever produced. Hall was hired by Green-Wood Cemetery 20 years earlier to produce a special six-volume set of over 150 albumen prints entitled *Gems from Green-Wood*. The cover page and one of the gems appear above.

Nine

Ballparks, "Bums," and Beyond

Ebbets Field was Brooklyn's most enduring monument to the national game for the first half of the 20th century, until the O'Malley family moved the borough's "beloved bums" out West and tore down the shrine to make way for high-rise apartments. Outside of the surviving outfield wall of old Washington Park on 3rd Avenue and the old Excelsior clubhouse on Clinton Street, few standing relics of Brooklyn's rich baseball history have endured. Only in the serene setting of Green-Wood have the monuments and graves of the legends themselves stood the test of time. It is fitting that when Ebbets Field was demolished in 1960, some of the dirt that Dodger players and their opponents once played upon was trucked to Green-Wood and scattered amid the graves of baseball's pioneers.

W. H. CAMMEYER DEAD.

Manager of the Old Union Grounds
Passes Away.

KNOWN TO WILLIAMSBURGHERS.

HIS DEMISE RECALLS A ONCE FA-
MOUS LOCAL RESORT.

Was a Pioneer Baseball Director Who
Did Much to Popularlize the
Game in Its Infancy.

William H. Cammeyer inherited his family's leather business in 1861. Soon after, he envisioned that the public might fancy the use of formal athletic grounds now that outdoor recreation was all the rage. Cammeyer leased property in Williamsburg hoping to create his own arena for local sports. He transformed the property as he enclosed it with a wooden fence and flooded the ground with water, creating what he called the Union Skating Pond. Cammeyer shrewdly chose to expand his operations with the establishment of the Union Base Ball Grounds. The idea made him baseball's first true entrepreneur.

William Cammeyer transformed his skating rink into a larger facility and planned to accommodate clubs like the Eckfords. By April 1862, the local papers were predicting Cammeyer's imminent success as he planned to charge a 10¢ admission to matches played upon his grounds. The Eckford, Putnam, and Constellation Clubs inaugurated the new grounds, and he offered the winning clubs prizes, such as bats and balls. Cammeyer operated his grounds in first-class fashion, and by May 15, 1862, they had become the game's first-ever permanent and enclosed baseball stadium and the first such stadium to charge admission. An early Union ticket is pictured here.

Cammeyer's success gave rise to Weed and Decker's Capitoline Grounds. Rueben Decker's father leased a farm in Bedford-Stuyvesant owned by Brooklyn's pioneer Lefferts family, and a portion of this land went to young Decker and his partner, Hamilton Weed. In the winter of 1862–1863, Weed and Decker established their Capitoline Skating Pond, and by 1865, they had expanded the scope of their operation to include a new baseball field. The Lefferts' burial grounds were located either close to or on the actual Weed and Decker property, and on May 31, 1865, possibly to make room for baseball, the remains of the Lefferts were moved to a plot in Green-Wood. The Green-Wood tombstone pictured belongs to John Lefferts, who was originally interred in the family burial grounds near Halsey Street. Decker and Weed would later be buried at Green-Wood.

Brooklyn's Union Grounds opened in 1862, and, in another baseball first, the patriotic Cammeyer hired a band to play the "Star Spangled Banner" before the start of the opening game. The ballpark provided Cammeyer the platform to establish a host of innovations in the game, which included groundskeeping, the sale of beverages, special days, prizes for clubs, and betting areas for gamblers. Within a decade, baseball had become a purely professional endeavor, and by 1875, Cammeyer had become the president of New York's Mutuals, a team long affiliated

with the infamous "Boss" Tweed of New York's Tammany Hall. The Union Grounds served as their home field. Cammeyer also became the club's manager for their inaugural season in the newly formed National League of 1876, posting a poor 21-35 record. Within no time, Cammeyer and his club were dropped from the professional circuit. By 1879, the Union Grounds were in disrepair, with sections of fences falling down in some places. It was a far cry from Cammeyer's first four seasons of operation, when he sold $583,650 worth of tickets.

Billie Barnie was considered a crafty baseball mind who managed to keep himself in the game for decades. He was one of the most quotable baseball men of his day and a favorite of the baseball press. Barnie survived in the game, in part, because of his knack for keeping an eye on club finances. Over the years, he journeyed to towns both large and small compiling a lifetime managerial record of 632 wins and 810 losses.

Barnie went to Hartford as a minor-league manager in 1899, but his health was failing, and on July 15, 1900, he died of asthmatic bronchitis. "Bald Billie" was buried at Green-Wood with a proper Masonic ceremony. His brother, Alexander, was buried in Green-Wood as a Civil War hero and commander of Brooklyn's storied 14th Regiment. Barnie was buried in the Paterson family plot pictured here.

As the son of a prominent New York builder, "Bald Billie" Barnie began his career in 1873 with the Brooklyn Atlantics and afterwards joined the Hartford Club of the National Association as their catcher in 1874. For the next decade, Barnie kicked around the country as a relatively mediocre talent, and by the mid-1880s, he found his own niche as a manager for the Baltimore Club in the American Association. But, after nine years with the club, the best his team ever finished was third place. In 1897, Charles Ebbets and the owners of the Brooklyn National League club gave Bald Billie a shot to manage their club, but all he could manage was a tie for sixth place. He never won the elusive National League pennant that he hoped for.

Copyright, 1899, by Gardiner, Fulton St., Brooklyn.

1—Ebbets 2—Hanlon 3—Dahlen 4—Kelly 5—Jennings 6—Yeager 7—Jones 8—Keeler 9—Hughes 10—McJames 11—Farrell 12—Kennedy 13—Casey 14—McGuire 15—Anderson 16—Dunn 17—Daly

BROOKLYN BASE BALL CLUB,
CHAMPIONS NATIONAL LEAGUE, 1899.

After Ebbets's own dismal managerial debut in 1898, he struck a deal with Baltimore owner Harry Von der Horst, which gave each man part ownership in the Brooklyn and Baltimore clubs simultaneously. Brooklyn raided the Baltimore talent, adding manager Ned Hanlon and premier players such as Joe Kelley, Willie Keeler, and Hughie Jennings to their roster. By the close of their first season together in 1899, they had captured their first pennant.

Long before he achieved prominence in the affairs of Brooklyn baseball, Charles Ebbets helped draft plans for Niblo's Garden, a famous 19th-century recreation center. He was also an avid fan of bowling and aspired to the political life, serving both as a member of the board of aldermen and a New York State assemblyman. His only political defeat was in his run for a state senate seat.

In 1883, Charles Byrne partnered with Joseph J. Doyle and Ferdinand A. Abell to form the professional Brooklyn club. They played on grounds where Washington's Revolutionary army fought and fittingly named their home field Washington Park. Byrne hired Charles Ebbets to hawk tickets and scorecards while he tended to multiple club duties. Ebbets worked his way up the ladder and, through club partner George Chauncey's generosity, began purchasing club stock in the 1890s. In 1898, he was elevated to club president and controlled the club's bookkeeping, as evidenced on the ledger page pictured here written in Ebbets's own hand c. 1899. Ebbets oversaw every detail of the operation down to how many peanuts were sold at the park.

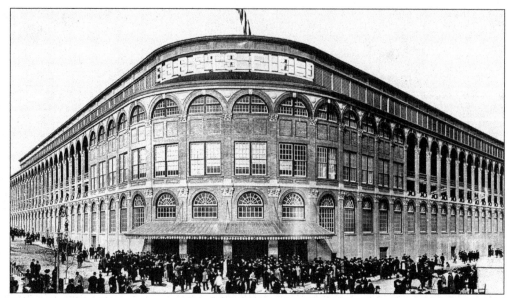

After several lackluster years at the club's Washington Park ticket windows, Ebbets yearned for a new ballpark to better serve the citizens of Brooklyn. So, in September 1908, he picked out the unlikely section of Flatbush known as "Pig Town" and began secretly buying up parcels of land sufficient to house a new ballpark. Although his team continued to struggle, Ebbets slowly acquired the land for the site of his ballpark and finally broke ground on March 4, 1912. Unfortunately, Ebbets ran into serious financial difficulties in the midst of construction and was forced to take on Brooklyn construction magnates Steven and Edward McKeever as partners. With their assistance and the infusion of $100,000 capital, Ebbets Field was completed in time for the opening of the 1913 baseball season.

Close to 50 years after Ebbets's 1913 grand opening, the stadium fell victim to the wrecking ball. Pictured here, longtime Dodger fan Ed Pinto looks on as the original cornerstone is broken open with a sledgehammer. Ebbets had dedicated the stadium to his son, Charles Jr., in 1913, but their relationship, too, was destroyed by the time Ebbets Sr. died. Young Charlie was denied his inheritance and died penniless. He was not even allowed burial in the family plot at Green-Wood.

The day of Ebbets's funeral was a gloomy, blustery one. Baseball's commissioner Judge Kenesaw Mountain Landis and fellow Hall of Famer Ban Johnson sullenly made their way through the cemetery with Ebbets's surviving partners, Edward and Steven McKeever, braving the elements to pay their last respects at his grave located on a hilltop known to be the highest point in Brooklyn.

Brooklyn's bad luck did not end with the death of Ebbets, as his partner Edward McKeever caught a nasty cold that day at Green-Wood and was thereafter confined to his bed until pneumonia set in. Tragically, at 66 years of age, McKeever died, marking the loss of two of the Brooklyn club owners in just 11 days. Steven McKeever assumed full control of the club and elected future Hall of Famer Wilbert "Uncle Robbie" Robinson as club president.

Currier and Ives produced thousands of lithographic titles featuring 19th-century subject matter ranging from railroading to horseracing. The firm fed the public's appetite for cheap and popular prints, and in 1865, they printed a baseball lithograph depicting the "Grand Match for the Championship at the Elysian Fields, Hoboken." Little did they know they would someday join their subjects who played for the Atlantic and Mutual Clubs at Green-Wood Cemetery. John C. Chapman appears as the batsman at the plate for the Atlantics, and Charles Smith leads off first base, while his teammates, grouped together on the first-base line, include Sidney Smith and Fred Crane. Mutuals Anson B. Taylor and John Wildey take their positions in the field, and the bearded "father of baseball," Henry Chadwick, appears in the small crowd of Brooklyn fans, looking directly at the viewer. (Courtesy of the National Baseball Hall of Fame Library, Cooperstown, New York.)

Long before Jackie Robinson and Branch Rickey broke baseball's color line in 1947, Nat C. Strong (a white booking agent) realized the potential in what was then known as the "colored baseball circuit." From the turn of the century until his death in 1935, Strong helped to establish the International League of Colored Base Ball Clubs. Over the years, he would battle black baseball pioneer and Hall of Famer "Rube" Foster for control of the black baseball leagues.

Nat Strong was a controversial figure in black baseball and was rumored to have swindled black owner John W. Connor out of control of his champion Brooklyn Royal Giants (pictured here c. 1917). Nonetheless, black baseball's first historian, Sol White, considered him one of the most important figures in black baseball history. Soon after his burial at Green-Wood in 1935, Strong's old partner, H. Walter Schlichter, remembered him as the only man who "made a million" in black baseball, but also added, "I am better off than he right now. I am still living and have my health, and Nat didn't take his wealth with him. There is no pocket in a shroud, you know."

Ernest Thayer's "Casey at the Bat" was published on June 3, 1888, but it was not until a fall evening later that year at Wallack's Theatre in New York that his poem would begin to become part of the fabric of American culture. Thespian DeWolf Hopper was given a clipping of the poem by his good friend Archibald Clavering Gunter. As the New York and Chicago ball clubs were in attendance for a performance of "Prince Methusalem," Hopper wanted to pay special tribute to the ballplayers whom he invited. Hopper delivered his first rendition of the poem during the first intermission. As he finished, a thunderous ovation erupted, and a baseball legend was born.

For the next half century, DeWolf Hopper repeated his performance well over 10,000 times, through the course of his six marriages, one of which was to Hollywood socialite Hedda Hopper. Hopper once boasted that he would be reciting "Casey at the Bat" on "resurrection morn," and, by 1935, he had recited his last. He was interred in his family plot at Green-Wood. Today, Hopper's legacy lives on in the performances of Cooperstown resident Tim Wiles, as he portrays the "Mighty Casey" and faithfully recites Thayer's verse at the National Baseball Hall of Fame inductions, all-star games, and even Memorial Day ceremonies at Green-Wood Cemetery. (Courtesy of the National Baseball Hall of Fame Library, Cooperstown, New York.)

While Green-Wood has a most storied history in terms of baseball's infancy and early development, it has at least one link to the modern game in its inclusion of legendary Brooklyn high school coach Frank "Chick" Keegan. In a career that began in the 1940s and spanned four decades, Keegan's most enduring legacy was as the high school coach of New York Yankee manager and six-time world champion Joe Torre.

Senior Joe Torre (standing in the center) appears with his Saint Francis Preparatory School teammates in a photograph that appeared in his 1958 yearbook. Under the watchful eye of manager Chick Keegan, Torre was the team's star player, winning the 1958 Powers Award for most valuable baseball player. Pictured kneeling right below Torre is the author's father, Ray Nash, Chick Keegan's trusty junior utility man and future assistant coach.

The significance of the Creighton monument at Green-Wood cannot be overstated. It was baseball's first off-field tourist destination and the game's first formal recognition of the greatness of one of its own. Creighton's recognition and the Excelsior Club's incorporation of baseball motifs above his grave laid the foundation for the game's long history of creating baseball legends through the symbolism of manmade monuments. The reverence felt by the early visitors to Creighton's monument mirrors similar sentiments felt by almost every New York fan who has strolled through Yankee Stadium's Monument Park.

The first reported pilgrimage to a sacred baseball site occurred in 1866, when Jim Creighton's teammates accompanied the National Club of Washington, D.C., to view his monument. Their pilgrimage illustrates the American penchant for creating symbolic icons to honor the past. Creighton's monument, admired and promoted in later years by the likes of Chadwick and Spalding, cultivated the game's awareness of its own history and contributed to the subsequent establishment of its own shrine in Cooperstown, New York. The atmosphere created in Cooperstown with the display of their Hall of Fame plaques is one of unmistakable deference and respect, no doubt an extension of the sentiments one might feel at the grave of a loved one or a childhood hero. Creighton was the game's first Hall of Fame caliber player, though he has never been officially recognized as such. Long before Cooperstown there was Green-Wood, and for more than 140 years it has served both the game and Creighton's memory well.

HENRY CHADWICK
BASEBALL'S PREEMINENT PIONEER
WRITER FOR HALF A CENTURY.
INVENTOR OF THE BOX SCORE.
AUTHOR OF THE FIRST RULE-BOOK
IN 1858. CHAIRMAN OF RULES
COMMITTEE IN FIRST NATION-WIDE
BASEBALL ORGANIZATION.

Visit us at
arcadiapublishing.com

CPSIA information can be obtained
at www.ICGtesting.com
Printed in the USA
LVOW01*1126040117
519696LV00014BA/145/P